Building Doors & Entryways

Building Doors & Entryways

Projects, Plans & Procedures

Craig Weis

Sterling Publishing Co., Inc.   New York
A Sterling/Lark Book

for Jessamyn and Karla
whose love opens so many new doors to our lives
KJH & CBW

Editor: Richard Freudenberger
Art Director: Kathleen Holmes
Photography: Evan Bracken
Production: Elaine Thompson and Kathleen Holmes
Illustrations: Don Osby

Library of Congress Cataloging-in-Publication Data
Weis, Craig, 1957–
    Building doors & entryways : projects, plans & procedures / Craig Weiss.
       p.   cm.
    "A Sterling/Lark book."
    Includes index.
    ISBN 0-8069-8168-7
    1. Wooden doors--Design and construction.   2. Doorways.
  I. Title
  TH2278.W45   1996
  694'.6--dc20   96-21290
                                     CIP

10 9 8 7 6 5 4 3 2 1

A Sterling/Lark Book

Published by Sterling Publishing Co., Inc.
  387 Park Ave. South, New York, NY 10016

Created and produced by Altamont Press, Inc.
  50 College St., Asheville, NC 28801

© 1996, Craig Weis

Distributed in Canada by Sterling Publishing, c/o Canadian Manda Group,
  One Atlantic Ave., Suite 105, Toronto, Ontario, Canada M6K 3E7

Distributed in Great Britain and Europe by Cassell PLC, Wellington House,
  125 Strand, London, England WC2R 0BB

Distributed in Australia by Capricorn Link (Australia) Pty Ltd.,
  P.O. Box 6651 Baulkham Hills Business Centre, NSW, Australia 2153

The projects in this book are the original creations of the contributing designers, who retain the copyrights to their designs. The projects may be reproduced by individuals for personal pleasure; reproduction on a larger scale with the intent of personal profit is prohibited. Every effort has been made to ensure that all the information in this book is accurate. However, due to differing conditions, tools, and individual skills, the publisher cannot be responsible for any injuries, losses, or other damages that may result from the use of the informationj in this book.

*Cover door: Craig Weis, author,
and owner of Architectural Woodcraft,
Asheville, North Carolina*

**Raised panel, loose-tenon construction
in white oak with Colonial maple-
red mahogany blend and varnish**
Photograph by Evan Bracken

CONTENTS

ACKNOWLEDGMENTS

ADDITIONAL PHOTOGRAPHS

Special thanks to John Brinkmann of American Bungalow who so generously provided the photographs of the Arts and Crafts doors on pages 8, 11, 109, 110, 120, 121, and 123. American Bungalow is published quarterly at 123 South Baldwin Avenue, Sierra Madre, CA 91024. Thanks, too, to Mr. Henry Lanz of the Garrett Wade Company who furnished the photograph on page 26.

LOCATION PHOTOGRAPHY

Personal thanks to Ivo, Django, and Lucy Ballentine and Robin Cape of Preservation Hall Antiques & Architectural Salvage in Asheville, North Carolina, who offered their time, home, and place of business to help bring this book to completion. Best of wishes for their newest venture in Weaverville, NC. Thanks, also, to Steve and Shirley Kayne and Jay Osborn of Kayne & Son Custom-Formed Hardware in Candler, NC for providing their workshop and handiwork. And particular thanks to the Cecil family and Lynn N. Hanson of Biltmore Estate in Asheville, NC, for their courtesy and indulgence in the Biltmore House photography. And of course, many thanks to the door owners in and around Asheville and Hendersonville, North Carolina who contributed so richly to this book:

Paige and Dean Alspaugh

The City of Asheville

Jessica Claydon of Touchstone Gallery

Janet and Andrew Hart

Doug Johnston of Wellstead Construction

Father Carl E. Kaltreider, Basilica of St. Lawrence DM

Robert Patton of Grovewood Gallery

Wayne Prine of Brightwater Art Glass

Rob Pulleyn, Publisher of Lark Books

T.W. Roberts

Amy Texido of The New French Bar

St. Mary's Parish Grove Park

Mary and Stephen Vieira

Anton Weber

Whalen Hay

Hugenschmidt Master and Devereux PA

Chip Worrell of Little River Woodworking

Michael Wrightson

And to: Bill Hamer of Forest Millwork, Inc. for opening his shop to us…to Joe Bruneau for his time and talent…to Tom Leslie of The Manor Inn for his support in the many restoration projects…to Sam W. Smith and David Monti for their woodworking help and expertise…and to Robbie Sweetser of R.S. Griffin Architects, P.A. in Asheville for all his restoration knowledge on doors in particular.

Doing a common thing uncommonly well often brings success.

A FRONT DOOR is much more than a means of access or a barrier against intruders. It's the first impression a visitor will get of a house and those living within it.

An entryway is designed to impress, and the door becomes the natural focus of this attention. A flicker of color, an unusual turn of molding, or a perfect match—whether architecturally, or merely in character with the house around it—is all it takes to distinguish a dreary slab of wood from something striking and wonderfully unique.

Doors are extraordinarily sturdy examples of the joiner's art, many dating from hundreds of years ago still in regular use. Yet, as intricate as they might seem to the woodworking novice, they don't have to be. A handful of construction techniques, in fact, are all that's needed to build a houseful of doors, all visibly different and delightfully functional.

Woodworking experience—or your lack of it—shouldn't be the pivot upon which your decision to build—or not build—your own door rests. This book was written so those who'd appreciate a unique door, inside or out of the house, would be able to have one regardless of their familiarity or skill with the fine points of woodworking.

With a small collection of hand tools, a few basic power tools, and a bit of patience, all of the core project doors in the pages that follow are within your reach. From that core group of doors, a multitude of variations make it possible for adventuresome novices to bring to life their own personal expression of what a door should be.

And if you're a regular hobby woodworker, all the better—you'll likely have access to the more sophisticated tools that can bring your project to fruition faster, though not necessarily any better, than the traditional bench assortment.

It's all here, from a doormaker's perspective. Beginners can get a helping hand with choosing their tools, planning a workshop, and using their equipment safely. Things like selecting the best wood for the job and choosing a design and building technique best suited to the situation are explained too. And finishing and embellishing the finished item are covered, as well.

And you'll even be let in on a few secrets: How many people do you know who can fit and hang a door correctly? What's the right way to fix a sticking or sagging door? How do you deal with an odd-sized opening, or one with less-than-conventional framing and trim? Which joint and fastening methods work the best?

Once you experience firsthand the sense of satisfaction possible from making a doorway something special and unique to you and yours alone, you'll never think about a ready-made door again.

Previous page: An unusually wide Grovewood Gallery eight-light frame-and-batten oak door with double-Z bracing and vertical beaded panels.

The entry door of this bungalow-style home offers a welcome change from the pedestrian, mass-produced look of store-bought doors.

THE RIGHT START

CHAPTER 1
OPENING A DOOR

WHAT YOU INTEND to do with this book is entirely up to you. You may have been intrigued by the possibilities of building your own door. You may have been taken by the wealth of distinctness and creativity exhibited by the many craftsmen whose work appears within the pages. Or you may have simply been seeking a less conforming way of entering and leaving your home every day.

What I have intended to do with this book is to serve up a fairly involved woodworking discipline in easy-to-digest portions—so that you could, starting from scratch, build and embellish your own door with complete creative freedom.

There's always the assumption that the skills of doormaking are far too complicated to pass along on paper, especially to people who have limited woodworking experience. But that assumption doesn't take into account that building doors—like building most anything large and intimidating—is just a series of small steps. With that in mind, I had an agenda in writing this book: to give you everything possible to set you on the path to doorbuilding distinction.

Finding a common denominator in woodworking is always difficult—there are just too many skill levels to contend with. So I didn't try. Beginning with the next chapter, you'll find the very basics spelled out: planning and setting up your workshop, developing a safe and healthy attitude toward the work and equipment, and feeling your way through the fundamental techniques needed to get the basic jobs done.

I detailed and described all the conceivable tools that could be used to build the simplest to most complex doors, setting aside only a few of the larger ones that seemed a bit unnecessary. Related things—the glues, fasteners, sanding and finishing techniques, hardware overviews, and the like—are addressed in individual chapters, along with installing locks, hanging and adjusting, and designing entryways.

Getting those matters out of the way then lays the groundwork for the stuff of creative doorbuilding—selecting wood with just the right color and grain…reflecting on the possibilities of custom millwork…appreciating the wealth of architectural salvage…and understanding that although there are a few rules of play, many of them can be bent enough to allow you to truly enjoy yourself.

Yes, once you're comfortable with the idea that a door is really a variety of elements—joints, frames, shapes, and moldings—that can be put together in almost any way imaginable, there will suddenly be a door opened for you—one that may free you to discard without guilt every factory-stamped, cookie-cutter slab-on-hinges that you own and replace it with an expression in wood of what ought to have been in the first place.

Previous page: A Grovewood Gallery frame-and-batten utility door with X-bracing and vertical beaded panels. The kick rail appears to have been modified and covered, perhaps because of work to the sill and threshold.

Opposite page: An arts-and-crafts door built in typical craftsman style. The use of oak, fir, and hard pine species can turn a weekend project into a work of art if done with care.

CHAPTER 2

THE WELL-PLANNED WORKSHOP

JUST FOR A MOMENT, never mind what kind of woodworking experience you have. Whether you're a rank beginner, an part-time dabbler, or a dedicated hobbyist, you can learn in a few paragraphs what sometimes takes even professional woodworkers many seasons to catch on to. That, in a word, is organization.

Believe it or not, the arrangement of your tools—and their relationship to your work and storage areas—is more of a key to productivity than how many machines or how much space you have. The pros know that time is money—their jobs flow smoothly, they work with fewer footsteps, and they avoid doing things twice. If money is lost, it's likely to be more for poor buying and selling skills than for lack of planning.

But in the amateur's case, time is pleasure. When the work goes smoothly, it's accompanied by pride and a sense of accomplishment. As confidence builds, so does the measure of safety and the quality of the project. It's an encouraging cycle, and one that quite naturally develops the experience that goes hand in glove with productivity.

There's always one risk in all this. It's too easy to be lured by the appeal of new tools and gadgets that you probably don't need. A word to the wise: Avoid the temptation. You'll find that beginning on as basic a level as possible will not only save you money, but will also allow you, as a woodworker, to become more proficient with the tools you do have at your disposal; witness some of the finest examples of wood craftsmanship created two centuries ago using hand tools crude by today's standards. Also, keep in mind that few tools take up less room than many, allowing you to make use of a smaller space, or one that may not have an ideal shape.

Following this train of thought, you can make improvements as need or finances permit, but don't be recklessly over-ambitious in your efforts. And try not to make major changes all at once. A good rule to follow is to give serious thought to a new tool candidate before even considering its purchase—not so much with regard to what it does, strictly, but more to how you plan to use it in the flow of things in your shop, and, in a practical sense, where it will fit in your work area's physical floor plan.

EVALUATING QUALITY SPACE

If you already have a workshop set up and you're comfortable with it, you still might want to just skim through this chapter for ideas to file in the back of your mind. There's always something to learn from other people's experiences, and the building of doors—

A sturdy workbench, adequate storage, and enough room to move around the tools are a few of the elements that help to define a good work space.

Opposite page: A new stained glass panel by Chris Juedemann set into a salvaged heart pine office door.

being a woodworking specialty with its own quirks and kinks—may require some modifications or additions you hadn't thought of.

Those who don't have an area dedicated to woodworking projects have a good opportunity to set up a workable space. Size isn't the most important factor. If you can swing a length of

wood in the room, you've got a good start. Of far more consequence is the quality of what's available.

The area should be dry for the sake of your tools and hardware. Also, wood and grain swell in a damp environment, and any stored stock might suffer under such conditions. Also, think of your comfort. Though working in an unheated shop is a real character-builder, there are still likely to be long stretches during which your tools lie idle. Temporary fixes such as portable space heaters are a solution, but not much of one. Fire safety in the presence of floating sawdust particles and finishing volatiles is just a hope. And the exhaust fumes from some types of fuel-oil heaters can affect the quality of your project's finish.

Ventilation is especially important if you don't have the luxury of a dust collection system, or you plan on doing substantial finishing work. A dust collector will not clear the air of harmful volatiles, but it will remove sawdust particles at the cutting source. A ventilating fan will help in removing dust in suspension and the fumes from drying finishes.

Lighting? It should be from overhead and preferably fluorescent. Diffusers—the grates or covers you see over fluorescent tubes—can be a problem in collecting dust, but are recommended because they protect the fragile glass tubes from the hazards of being struck by flying wood chunks. Ambient natural light is fine if it's available, but most wood shops don't have that luxury. (Besides, wall space occupied by a window is storage space lost.) Task, or spot, lighting is advantageous with certain fine-operation tools such as a scroll or band saw simply because you can easily see where the blade is going.

Security is a concern as well, not only from thieves but from curious children who could hurt themselves on sharp edges, or be tempted by power equipment. Doors should be stable and preferably locked with a deadbolt or padlock, and entry areas clear and visible. Also, as obvious as it may seem, at least one access must be large enough to accommodate a finished door project—a requirement that might only be difficult to meet in a basement workshop with a tight stairwell.

And, speaking of power, your shop's electrical service should be adequate for the tools at hand. Tool outlets should be on a separate circuit from lighting, and all breakers must be functional and the grounds complete. A large stationary tool such as a table saw or surface planer may have higher voltage and amperage needs and if that's the case it should have its own dedicated circuit.

Tools and Work Flow

As in any woodworking endeavor, making doors requires a basic selection of stationary tools, and for the sake of discussion let's say those include a table saw, a radial arm (or sliding compound miter) saw, a band saw, a drill press, and a workbench. You may not think of the bench as a tool, but it certainly functions as one and will occupy space on your floor.

RECTANGULAR SHOP PLAN

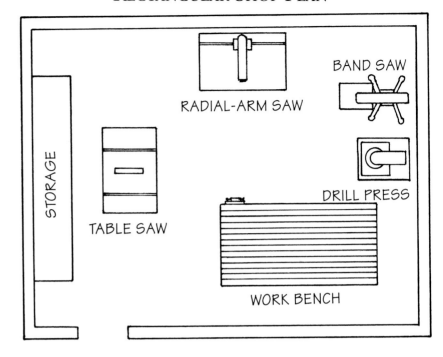

FIGURE 1

NARROW SHOP PLAN

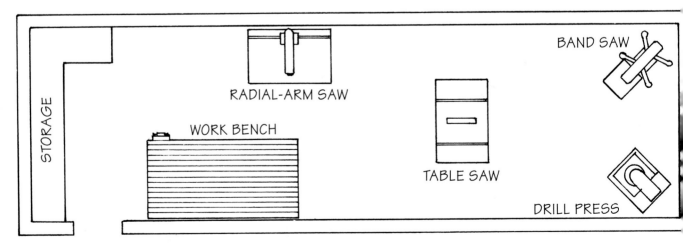

FIGURE 2

As you develop your door-making skills (politely assuming you may be just starting) you'll find there are specific tools and procedures that you prefer. Let this awareness and the common sense of your work's natural flow guide you in setting up or modifying your work space.

The work will move you from tool to tool, and this movement must be fluid and logical. To establish the best work flow, it's important to realize that woodworkers move between three major areas—tool and material storage, stationary tool sites, and the workbench. If these elements are arranged in a triangular pattern, you'll have an open space in the center that'll allow you to move unobstructed from point to point.

Naturally, the shape of your workshop will dictate the boundaries of your triangle. A square or rectangular space (see Fig. 1) is probably the most practical to set up and work in. The workbench is best placed near the longest wall, and the standing tools against two adjacent walls. The remaining wall can be used for storage. Remember that both the table saw and workbench require some walking space around them to allow reasonable access. A drill press or a radial arm saw, on the other hand, can be backed up against a wall, though there should be some working clearance at the sides.

A long and narrow space as shown in Fig. 2 may force you to break the triangular work pattern. In a situation such as this, an in-line flow pattern can function perfectly well, as long as the workbench is centrally located so it becomes the point from which your movement to tools and storage takes place. Even if you must put the bench against a wall, you'll still be able to work it from three sides. And if you're careful to place the items you use most frequently—the hand-held power tools, clamps, and measuring tools, for

example—nearest the workbench and the middle of the shop, you're bound to increase your efficiency.

Doormaking sometimes requires a second workbench, and that can complicate things a bit. Often, a folding or collapsible work surface can function as a workbench and then be set aside when it's not needed. Another practical approach is to set up mobile work stations. By installing locking wheels to the base of a table saw, for instance, it can be easily and temporarily moved out of the work-flow zone when it's not needed, and a second work surface can go in its place. The radial arm or sliding compound miter saw can be used in its absence.

WHAT'S THE BEST WORKBENCH?

The answer to that question is simple if you're a general woodworker—it's a stable and sturdy surface that holds all the components while you assemble your project. It'll include a vise or at least a means of clamping down your work, and a tray or drawer to keep necessary tools and materials within reach. For comfort, the top should be about 4 inches below your waist.

Assembling a door, however, asks for a bit more in the way of a workbench. The surface needs to be large, square, and perfectly flat to accommodate the layout and clamping chores you'll be faced with in a door project. While a traditional bench will work for a lot of preparation tasks and can even be rigged for door-clamping, another option is open to the enterprising doormaker, and that is to use an unwarped solid-core door at least 1-3/4 inches thick and 36 to 40 inches wide mounted to a sturdy set of legs.

The importance of a substantial base can not be overstated, simply because there's nothing quite so frustrating as laying into a stubborn screw or routing a temperamental edge while trying to

compensate for a table wobbling under the pressure. A stand (Fig. 3) made from 2 X 4s glued and fastened at the joints with No. 12 screws and restrained from racking by the use of perimeter bands, diagonal cross-bracing, and 3/4-inch shelf platforms takes a few hours to construct—time very well spent.

Another approach might be just the ticket for someone who needs a mobile work surface. The true door bench shown in Fig. 4 is a framework compact and lightweight enough to be moved between rooms. It's a traditional bench used by carpenters to support doors of various sizes while planing and fitting hinges and locksets. The main feature of this bench is the adjustable clamp setup used for holding the door on edge, a bonus for busy carpenters, yet not entirely useless to a hobbyist. Recessed tool wells at the ends also offer a convenient spot to keep hand and power tools. It, too, can be furnished with a surplus-door top and used as a workbench or table.

A Shop-Built Workbench

When is a door not a door? When it's a workbench. To make this sturdy stand, you'll need the standard dimensional lumber indicated in the list below, a few hand tools, and, of course, a door. For strength, choose a construction-grade wood species such as spruce, fir, or pine—hardwood isn't necessary. Be sure to work on a level floor when you build or the work surface won't be on an even plane.

Suggested Tools

Circular or table saw

3/8" Variable-speed drill

No. 8 screw bit

No. 12 screw bit

Phillips screwdriver bit

Tape measure

Combination square

Pipe or bar clamps

Caulk gun

Cut List

6	Legs	1-1/2" X 3-1/2" X 32-1/2"
4	Ends	1-1/2" X 3-1/2" X 21"
2	Mid braces	1-1/2" X 3-1/2" X 21"
4	Sides	1-1/2" X 3-1/2" X 72"
1	Diagonal	1-1/2" X 3-1/2" X 76"
2	Shelves	3/4" X 24" X 32"

Hardware and Supplies

No. 12 X 3" flathead wood screws

No. 8 X 1-1/2" flathead wood screws

2" Angle brackets

Construction adhesive

Solid-core 1-3/4" door

Construction Procedure

1. Set two of the legs parallel on a flat surface, wide faces down and 14" apart. Mark 4" from the lower end of both pieces. Center one end piece with its lower edge on these marks, and center a second end piece with its upper edge flush with the top of the legs. Use the No. 12 screw bit to drill two diagonally placed holes 2-1/2" deep at each of the four joints. Apply adhesive and fasten the joints with No. 12 X 3" screws.

2. Repeat this procedure with two more ends and legs. On the third or middle set, attach the mid braces to opposite faces of the legs.

3. Stand the three finished assemblies on their side edges, with each end set 32" from the middle set. Locate and mark the midpoint of two side pieces and center each one in line with the butts of the end pieces. Adjust the middle unit if needed to align with the midpoint of each side piece. Use the No. 12 screw bit to drill two holes 2-1/2" deep at each of the six joints. Fasten the joints with adhesive and No. 12 X 3" screws.

4. Lay the diagonal across the leg frames so it extends between the lower left and upper right corners. Mark the cut line at each end, using the outer face of the legs as a guide. Cut the ends of the diagonal at the marks. Use the square to check that the legs are perpendicular to the side pieces, then reposition the diagonal, clamp it, and drill three holes at each of the joints with the No. 12 screw bit. Fasten permanently with adhesive and No. 12 X 3" screws.

5. Turn the entire assembly over so it rests on the side you just worked on. Repeat Step 3 on the opposite side. Installing a second diagonal as in Step 4 is optional, and probably not necessary. (It will limit your access to the shelves as well.) If you choose to add the extra diagonal, mount it in the opposite direction from the first.

6. Set the bench up on its legs. Place the two plywood shelves in position on the top edges of the lower side pieces. Use the No. 8 screw bit to drill a series of holes about 5-1/2" apart and 1-1/2" deep through the plywood and into the side pieces. One of the shelves should also be match-drilled to the single lower mid brace. Apply adhesive to the drilled edges of the framing and attach the shelves with No. 8 X 1-1/2" screws.

7. Position the door on top of the bench so it's centered. Place the angle brackets at the upper ends of each leg so they meet the underside of the door face. Predrill the holes and use a pair of No. 8 X 1-1/2" screws to fasten each bracket to its leg. To secure the door, use one screw per bracket; this will make it easier to remove or reposition the top if needed. Avoid gluing the door to the surface of the workbench.

SHOP-BUILT WORKBENCH

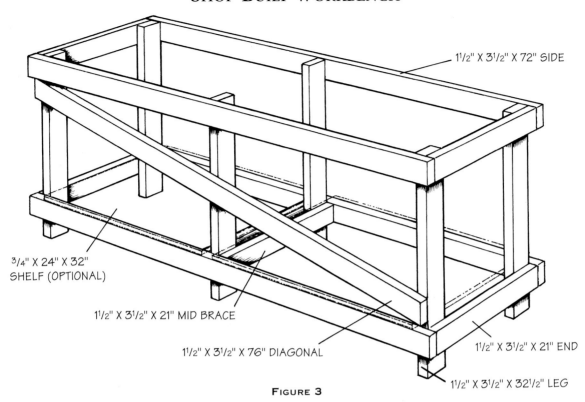

1¹/₂" X 3¹/₂" X 72" SIDE

3/4" X 24" X 32"
SHELF (OPTIONAL)

1¹/₂" X 3¹/₂" X 21" MID BRACE

1¹/₂" X 3¹/₂" X 76" DIAGONAL

1¹/₂" X 3¹/₂" X 21" END

1¹/₂" X 3¹/₂" X 32¹/₂" LEG

FIGURE 3

THE TRADITIONAL DOOR BENCH

You can make this door bench using dimensional lumber from a builder's supply yard. No. 2 pine or the equivalent will work for both the 1 X 4 and 2 X 4 pieces. This is more of a work table than a bench, so it needn't be built to take a pounding—screw joints are adequate. The lower rests can be moved up or down to accommodate different width doors on edge, and the clamp adjusted right or left to secure the door against the side of the bench. As with the accompanying workbench, you can make this bench even more useful by adding a top made from an old door.

CUT LIST

4	Legs	1-1/2" X 3-1/2" X 32"
2	Sides	3/4" X 3-1/2" X 72"
2	Side rails	3/4" X 3-1/2" X 72"
2	Ends	3/4" X 7-1/2" X 22-1/2"
2	End rails	3/4" X 3-1/2" X 22-1/2"
2	Mid braces	3/4" X 7-1/2" X 22-1/2"
2	Shelves	3/4" X 20" X 22-1/2"
2	Rests	3/4" X 3-1/2" X 26-1/2"
1	Clamp	3/4" X 3-1/2" X 27-1/2"
1	Stop	3/4" X 1-1/2" X 3-1/2"

SUGGESTED TOOLS

Circular or table saw

Jigsaw

3/8" Variable-speed drill

No. 8 screw bit

No. 10 screw bit

Phillips screwdriver bit

Tape measure

Combination square

Pipe or bar clamps

HARDWARE AND SUPPLIES

No. 10 X 2" flathead wood screws

No. 8 X 1-1/2" flathead wood screws

CONSTRUCTION PROCEDURE

1. Lay two of the legs parallel on a flat surface 15-1/2" apart. Mark 4" from the lower end of both pieces. Place the lower edge of one of the end rails at this point and place one of the wider ends so its upper edge is flush with the top of the legs. Use a No. 10 screw bit to drill three holes along each end of the upper piece and two holes at each end of the lower rail. Fasten with No. 10 X 2" screws.

2. Repeat this procedure with the remaining two legs, rails, and end pieces.

3. Stand the assemblies upright and 6 feet apart. Position one of the 72" side pieces against the sides of the leg assemblies so its upper edge is flush with the top of the legs. Clamp it in position and drill two diagonally placed holes into each joint using a No. 10 screw bit. Fasten with No. 10 X 2" screws.

4. Attach one of the 72" side rails to the lower part of the leg frame so it aligns with the end rails, using the procedure described in Step 3.

5. Repeat this procedure on the opposite side of the bench with the remaining side and rail pieces.

6. Measure 21-1/8" from the corner of each end board and mark at the top edge of the side pieces. Center a mid brace at each of these points and clamp. Use a No. 8 screw bit to drill two holes at each joint, and fasten the braces with No. 8 X 1-1/2" screws.

7. Place one shelf board at each end, at the top of the bench, and scribe around the legs with a pencil. Cut out the corners with a jigsaw, then slide the shelves down until they're flush with the lower edge of the ends and braces. Use No. 8 X 1-1/2" screws placed 5-3/8" apart to fasten the vertical parts to the edges of the shelves.

8. Fasten the stop to one end of the clamp with two No. 8 X 1-1/2" wood screws. This bar and the two rests at the lower part of the bench are fastened to the table with C-clamps. The rests can be moved up or down and the clamp sideways to accomodate different sized doors.

DOOR BENCH

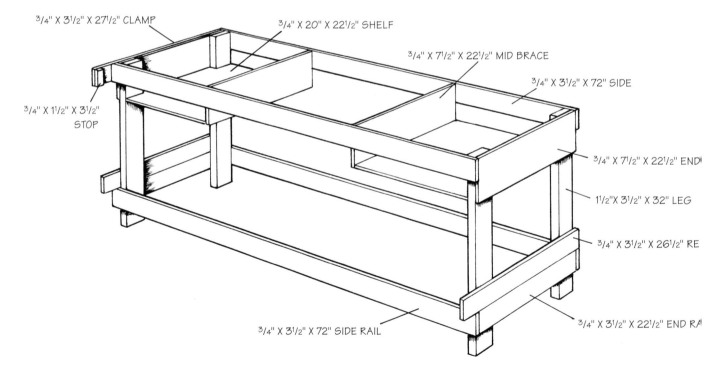

3/4" X 3¹/2" X 27¹/2" CLAMP

3/4" X 20" X 22¹/2" SHELF

3/4" X 7¹/2" X 22¹/2" MID BRACE

3/4" X 3¹/2" X 72" SIDE

3/4" X 1¹/2" X 3¹/2" STOP

3/4" X 7¹/2" X 22¹/2" END

1¹/2"X 3¹/2" X 32" LEG

3/4" X 3¹/2" X 26¹/2" RE

3/4" X 3¹/2" X 72" SIDE RAIL

3/4" X 3¹/2" X 22¹/2" END RA

FIGURE 4

CHAPTER 3

WOODWORKING TECHNIQUES: KNOW YOUR BASICS

THIS CHAPTER IS for those who may be new to woodworking. It's a general description of the tool-working techniques described throughout the book, along with some definitions of common woodworking terms. You should refer to Chapter 4 for information on specific tools. The individual door projects discussed later will also include suggestions for dealing with specific procedures that come up in building those projects.

If your woodworking skills are minimal, you can get comfortable with the terminology and pick up new techniques by studying this section carefully. More experienced woodworkers can review it, too, if only to brush up on techniques that are often taken for granted. Even the experts might learn a few tricks special to doormaking but not generally circulated.

MEASURING: RIGHT THE FIRST TIME

Careful measurement and layout is a fundamental element of good woodworking. But regardless of how many times you recheck your measurements, you'll still be off if you use the wrong tool. You don't use a 6" rule to measure a 10' distance, and you shouldn't expect a 16' tape to mark a fine mortise accurately. More important, you should stick with the same tools through the completion of the project—switching tapes or marking gauges in midstream is just an invitation to small mistakes.

Usually, the steel tape is considered the basis of the measuring game. Most general measuring jobs fall to the steel tape because it's fast and accurate within

1/16"—acceptable for almost any but the finest of woodworking projects.

But a steel tape can't strike a straight line over any distance. The metal band will move or distort no matter how careful you are. For distances less than 36", then, a straightedge is the best choice if you need to mark a line greater than an inch or so in length.

As an option, you can always use a chalk line—a chalked string stretched between two points—in a pinch, or you can use the tape to mark short increments over a greater distance, then strike lines between them with a straightedge if you have to.

When marking for a cut, purists may insist on avoiding pencils and using only a pointed steel scribe. Be that as it may, a sharp pencil can still make a very accurate V-shaped mark, which works well because the point of the V shows right where to cut.

Establishing a square or perpendicular edge is the job of a square. This is necessary for marking crosscuts or transferring a line to the remaining three sides of a board. A try square does the job best on smaller pieces, a framing square on the larger ones. Use it by laying the stock, or handle, of the tool against the edge of the work, and marking, in pencil, a line along the blade. To transfer the line to the side and back surfaces, walk the square around the work, using the tail of the previous line as the start of the next one, and so on.

To lay out a radius of partial or full circles, use a compass. Open its legs to the correct radius, then place the point at the center of the circle or arc you wish to make and swing the other leg to

make the mark. Remember that the radius is half a circle's width, while the diameter is its full width.

Figuring angles can be difficult, but the job is simplified with a protractor. The standard transparent type or the stainless steel engineer's kind with degree graduations along the edge are both fine. Lay the bottom along the work's baseline and the measurement can be read at the top arc. But the more sophisticated bevel protractor has a pivoting arm that can be laid alongside the angle as well, making it easier to read or establish the existing angle or bevel.

A level is used to establish the degree off "plumb" (straight up and down) or "level" (horizontally straight) of a framing member. The level's frame is laid against the side or top of the member, and the position of the bubble within the appropriate vial tells you how true the piece is. A centered bubble indicates perfect accuracy. For plumb measurement, the end vials are used; for determining level, the center one is read.

A straightedge encourages precise measurements where detail is important.

Clamps: Tighten with Care

Most of the clamps used in woodworking function to hold parts together while they're being glued. They can also secure pieces for cutting or drilling.

Bar or pipe clamps are especially suited for door-sized clamping jobs because they're long and relatively inexpensive for their size. A sliding tailpiece permits a large range of adjustment between the jaws. At least four or six are needed to keep a door square while gluing.

In the case of joints or pieces less than 12" in depth, a C-clamp is the logical choice. These clamps come in standard and deep throat depths, but they all have a threaded rod with a swivel tip that applies pressure to the work as you tighten the rod. You should cut some 2"-square pads from scrap pieces of 1/4" plywood to keep the metal tips from marring the face of your work.

The best results in joint-clamping come when you place the clamp's pressure points directly at the centerline of the work or joint to be glued. Snug-tightening is best, since over-tightening can damage the wood and, with gluing, force enough adhesive from the joint to cause uneven distribution and a weakened bond.

Cuts: Proceed with Caution

After you've done the measuring and marking, making the cuts is a matter of following the lines. Double-check your measuring work, because once a cut is made, the halves can't be made whole again.

When using a handsaw, grip it firmly—but not tensely—with the back of the handle squarely against the ball of your palm. Guide the teeth with the outer edge of your thumb when starting a cut, which should be made on the waste, or outer, side of the line. Except for some specialty saws, a cut is always started on the upstroke, and the blade

must be kept square with the surface of the wood.

With crosscuts, the tool should be held at a 45-degree angle, With rip cuts, the process works better at 60 degrees. The cutting pressure should be delivered only on the downstroke.

When using a circular saw, make sure the blade depth is set—by loosening a knob and moving the shoe up or down—so the teeth fully penetrate the opposite face of the work. This clears sawdust particles and makes the blade less likely to jam. Also, make sure your sawhorse or workbench is out of the way of the blade, or you'll cut it along with your work.

Top: Long clamps are used frequently in doormaking because of the outsized nature of the work.

Bottom: A table saw is used to cut the bevels on a raised panel.

■ HAND-CUTTING A MORTISE AND TENON ■

THE MORTISE

THE TENON

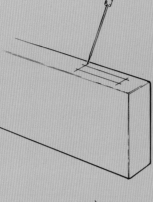

Step 1. Use a square and a knife or scratch awl to outline the layout of the mortise, or socket. It should be about one-third the thickness of the member itself.

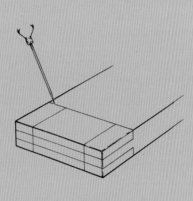

Step 1. Lay out the dimensions of the tenon with a marking gauge or square to match the mortise in thickness, length, and depth. Score the lines with a knife or scratch awl.

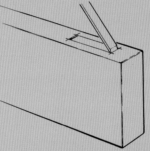

Step 2. Use a chisel or a sharp knife to score the wood on the lines. Then chisel out each end of the mortise slightly to a depth of about 1/8".

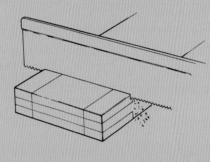

Step 2. Use a backsaw to cut the shoulders of the tenon evenly on both sides to the marked width.

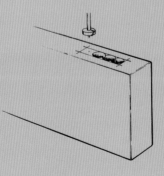

Step 3. Choose an auger or Forstner bit that equals the width, or slightly less, of your mortise. Drill a series of holes in line to a depth of at least one-third the width of the member.

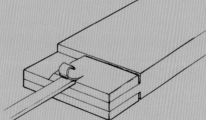

Step 3. Cut the sides of the tenon to the shoulder line with a sharp chisel.

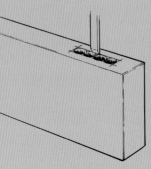

Step 4. Smooth and square the sides and ends of the mortise. Hold the chisel straight up and down, or angle it slightly into the wood to get a better bite if needed.

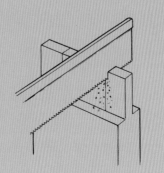

Step 4. Saw the tenon to the marked length right down to the shoulder line. Pare the high spots with a chisel if needed for fit.

Assume a comfortable position before starting the saw, but not one which will put you off balance at the end of a long cut. Don't grip the handle too tightly, because it'll make your hand tired and may throw off the accuracy of your work. The larger saws come with a second grip at the front for added control, but remember that two-handed sawing requires that you clamp your work down before cutting.

Always wear safety glasses when using any saw. Draw the power cord behind you before starting the tool, and sight your line of cut along the reference mark on the front of the saw's shoe. The safety guard will swing up by itself as you move the tool forward.

A table saw can cut more precisely because it has a guide fence and a miter gauge. The cutting depth is set with the handwheel located at the front of the saw cabinet; the blade should penetrate the work enough that several full teeth are exposed during the cut, as this cools the blade and allows the sawdust to escape.

To adjust the fence, loosen the lock and slide the fence to the right or left as needed. You can use the gauge on the fence rails for measuring the width of cut, but a more accurate method is to take a steel tape reading between the fence's edge and the tip of a blade tooth set toward the fence.

After starting the motor, allow it a few seconds to come up to speed—don't shove a piece of wood into a slowly moving blade. Never put your hands near the spinning blade; use a push stick to pass the work through.

A thin-bladed coping saw is the basic curve-cutting tool for thinner material and tight contours because it's easily controlled. If the stock is more than 3/8" or so in thickness, or the line greater than the throat depth of the saw, a hand-held electric jigsaw is the tool of choice. The tighter the curve or circle,

the thinner the jigsaw blade should be so it doesn't bind or overheat.

Cutting at an angle, as when making miters and bevels, can be done in several ways. A miter is an angle-cut made across the face of a board, as in the corners of a picture frame. A bevel is an angle cut into the edge of a board, as in a piece of trim or molding. And a compound cut is a combination of both. If the wood is less than 6" or so in width, a miter box used with a fine backsaw gives the most accurate miter cut.

The shoe on a circular saw can be adjusted to a 45-degree angle for bevel cutting. For greater accuracy, the table saw blade can be adjusted to the same degree by using the handwheel on the side of the cabinet.

To make a miter cut on the table saw, loosen the knob on the miter gauge and adjust its fence to the desired angle, then tighten the knob. By holding the work against the fence, both the gauge and the work can be moved forward to meet the blade.

Rabbets and grooves can be cut with a table saw fitted with a dado blade, though with many projects it's easier to make them using a router and a straight bit. To use the saw for this procedure, remove the table insert and set the dado head width. This can be done in one of two ways, depending on the blade design. The offset "wobbler" type has a rotating hub that changes the width by altering the degree of offset. The stacked type must be set up out of the saw and reinstalled on the arbor. When you stack the chippers between the outer blades, make sure that the teeth rest between the gullets of the adjacent blades and that the chippers are staggered around the circumference.

Adjust the depth of the blade with the handwheel and set the fence to establish the position of the rabbet or groove on the work.

GROOVES AND JOINTS: A CLOSE SHAVE

Mortised locks and hinges require that you clean up and straighten surfaces that haven't been completely cut with a saw or drill. This is a job for the chisel, and it's really not a challenge as long as you maintain the tool's sharp edge.

On most work, you won't even need to use a mallet; hold the tool in your right hand to provide the push, and guide the blade with the left to control direction. If you do use a mallet, strike the tool lightly so as to avoid taking big bites at once. Work with the grain and hold the tool at a slight angle (right or left) whenever possible, because this provides the smoothest cut and is less likely to dull the blade. To avoid gouging the work, don't drive the edge too steeply. Instead, hold the blade level or just at a slight downward angle.

For deeper cuts or shaping work, a router can handle quickly and cleanly what would take a far longer time with a saw and chisel. The shape of the router bit's cutting surfaces determine what the finished edge or groove will look like. A straight bit makes a slot the width of the bit itself; a roundover

A clean dado can be cut quickly and accurately with a router and slot-cutting bit.

bit cuts a clean, rounded edge into a squared surface; a chamfer bit cuts a beveled edge; and a ogee cuts a detailed profile.

When operating a router, you should grasp it comfortably in both hands and position yourself to get a clear look at the working bit—be sure to wear eye protection. The rule is to move the router from left to right; if circular or irregular cutting is required, then the motion should be counterclockwise. It's best to make any cuts across the end grain of your work first, then with the grain to avoid chipping.

The base of the router can be loosened and the motor housing adjusted up or down to control the depth of cut. Before making any permanent cuts, you should run a test on a piece of scrap wood to see what your work will look like. Practice will improve your control of the tool, and after a while, you'll be able to rely on the depth gauge marked on the side of the router rather than test every cut you make.

Freehand work is fine for short jobs, or when the bit has an attached pilot bearing, but when cutting long dadoes and grooves, you'll probably need to clamp the wood to a bench and use the tool's base-mounted guide to keep the cut straight. If you don't have a guide, you can usually substitute by clamping a straight section of 1 X 2 to the bench or your work, parallel to the line of cut.

Routing narrow stock or edge-rabbeting grooves will require that you place a piece of scrap stock to the right and left of the work, flush with the working surface. This will prevent the router base from tilting to one side and spoiling the cut, and will give you a place to mount a guide if you use one.

DRILLING: A PERFECT BORE

A screw hole consists of three parts: the pilot or lead hole (which is a little more than half the diameter of the screw itself), the shank or body hole (the same diameter as the screw), and the sink or bore, used if the screw head is to be recessed below the surface of the wood.

In softwoods, it's not really necessary to drill more than just the pilot hole for a short screw. Dense hardwoods and long screws may require that you drill the shank hole, too. Make that hole only as deep as the shank—the unthreaded portion of the screw—is long. Also, remember that screws driven into wood's end grain have less than half the holding power of a screw driven perpendicular to the grain.

Combination countersink/pilot bits, called screw bits, simplify hole-drilling considerably. They're sized by screw numbers, and their stop collars and countersinks are adjustable for length. They use specially tapered bits that accommodate standard wood screws perfectly.

Where appropriate (in softwoods, for No. 6 and No. 8 diameters), self-tapping power-driven screws—sometimes called drywall or cabinet screws—are even more convenient, though you should take care to predrill the pilot holes when driving screws near the end of the wood. A third variation known as deck screws are coated with a smooth anodization that makes them weather resistant. They'll work in hardwoods, but the screw holes must be predrilled at all times or you run the risk of splitting the wood or shearing the screw head off when the fastener is driven deeply in place.

Boring sockets can be done with a regular drill bit if the diameters are small enough—1/4" or 3/8". A hole larger than that needs a Forstner bit, which produces a clean, flat-bottomed hole.

A power auger bit creates the sockets for the start of a loose-tenon joint.

A stop collar can be used on a standard drill bit if you feel you may have trouble gauging the depth of a socket accurately.

Drilling through-holes and bores requires some care in not tearing out the back side of the work, especially if another piece is planned to face it. You can avoid splintering wood this way by drilling only partially through the piece, then coming at the hole from the opposite side. Using a small pilot bit to penetrate the back face helps to locate the point at which to start the second bore.

SAFETY

Power tools can be dangerous if misused. Carelessness, haste, and sheer ignorance are equal in the eyes of the saw—it will cut whatever gets in its way regardless of why it's there. Actually, just about any tool has the potential for causing injury. Some can merely do it more quickly or more effectively than others. The edge of a well-honed chisel can slice in a heartbeat, and you may not even know it; conversely, the blade of a radial arm saw can throw a chunk of wood into an unprotected eye with immediate results. Even sawdust, over time, can seriously damage your respiratory system.

■ COMMON RAIL AND STILE JOINTS ■

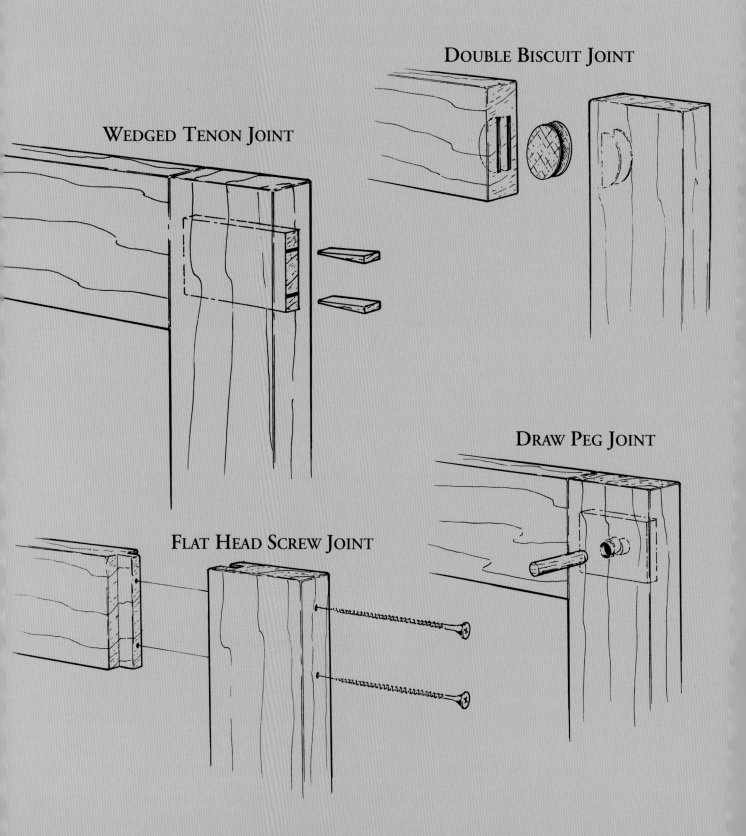

DOUBLE BISCUIT JOINT

WEDGED TENON JOINT

DRAW PEG JOINT

FLAT HEAD SCREW JOINT

■ COMMON RAIL AND STILE JOINTS ■

MORTISE AND TENON JOINT

DOWEL JOINT

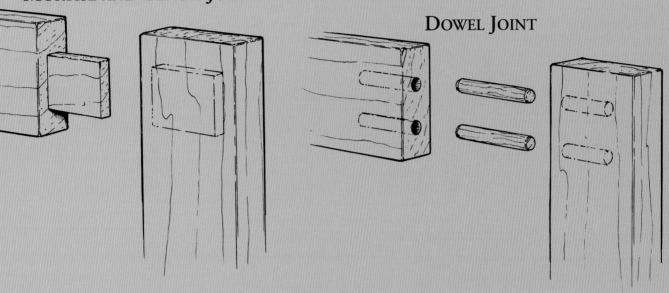

LOOSE TENON JOINT

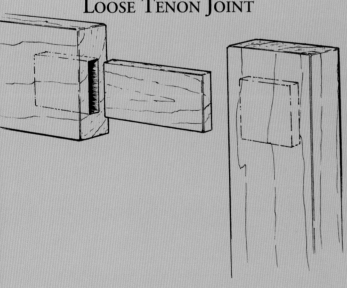

TONGUE AND GROOVE JOINT

This is not to present an argument for packing away your woodworking hobby. A wood shop, carefully laid out and treated with respect, can be as safe as your home's kitchen. The following guidelines will help you in establishing those rules that are so important to your health and well-being.

~ Dress appropriately for the work you're doing. Loose cuffs and shirt sleeves, untied long hair, and hanging jewelry are just invitations to an accident.

~ Keep your mind on your work, and be alert to what's going on around you. Distractions are not only an immediate hazard, but can have later repercussions, too. An interruption while tightening a saw blade or router bit may cause you to leave the job unfinished—your "reminder" could be in the form of a disaster when you next use the tool.

~ Unplug all power tools when making adjustments or changing blades and bits. This applies not only to hand tools such as routers and circular saws, but to stationary tools as well.

~ Clean and tidy are the watchwords of the wood shop. Work surfaces cluttered with extraneous tools, extension cords lying loose or stretched across the floor, and stashes of lumber leaning precariously here and there not only take time to maneuver around, but also invite slips, trips, and falls.

~ Leave blade guards and other safety features in place while you work. It's tempting to remove those additions (and in some special circumstances even necessary), but it's best to learn how to work with them. A piece of metal or high-impact plastic will take a chip of wood or a fragment of steel better than you will.

~ Always wear safety glasses or goggles. Glass or polycarbonate lenses must be impact resistant; goggles are preferred over glasses because they provide protection at the sides of the eyes as well as

at the front. Full-face shields are also worth considering. Ear protection, too, is important in a noisy shop environment. Over-the-head muffs which reduce decibel levels by at least 25 dB are recommended, especially when working with noisy tools such as routers, saws, planers, and sanders.

~ Dust protection should be more than just an option. Disposable dust masks are better than nothing at all, but a quality mask can be comfortable and filter particles down to the recommended .5-micron level as well. For finishing work, where exposure to solvents and vapors can be a real concern, a true respirator, complete with .3-micron-level filter cartridges, is an inexpensive investment. Both masks together cost about the same as a high-quality carbide saw blade. In general, dust in the shop can be greatly reduced through the use of a dust collector connected by hose to each source—table saw, shaper, etc.—and kept under control by a window fan in the summer and a reasonably priced recirculating filtration system through the heating season.

~ Don't bring an open flame into the wood shop. Cigarettes, pipes, and lighters are best left outside the work area. If you heat your shop with a space heater or furnace on-site (not through ductwork or radiators from elsewhere), keep in mind that flammable vapors from solvents, paints, and finishes are potentially combustible if left unvented. A 10-pound, A-B-C rated, dry-chemical fire extinguisher should be on hand in any case.

~ Working on damp or wet floors can be an electrical, as well as a physical, hazard. All your tools should be double-insulated, and the ground circuit in your shop's wiring should be functional.

~ Do what's necessary to protect your shop from curious youngsters. Unplug tools or shut off circuit breakers if the shop is accessible, otherwise lock the workshop up. Children can be taught woodworking and its safety, but that's a one-on-one education process that should be put off until the child is ready to follow directions and take some responsibility.

Eye, ear, and respiratory protection should be mandatory even in a home wood shop.

CHAPTER 4

HAND AND POWER TOOLS

Successful doormaking is based on access to a collection of hand and power tools, in addition to a few stationary tools.

THIS CHAPTER IS an overview of the tools you might use in doormaking—either to complete the projects in the book or to build doors of your own design and style. Don't be intimidated by the number of tools listed—they're not all needed, but every one could be used.

If you're a relative newcomer to woodworking, take the time to review the whole chapter closely, not only for safety's sake, but to better understand what each tool is capable of doing. An investment in tools can be considerable, and, while you certainly don't need every one mentioned, you will need a basic stable of workhorses to get the job done.

Those familiar with wood will probably recognize that some of the tools listed are there to make the job at hand go more quickly or easily. A brisk cadence may be essential in a production shop, where time is money and money is prosperity, but a hobby woodworker should have the luxury of enjoying the work and the freedom to experiment a bit as well. On the other hand, certain plug-in tools have that remarkable ability to turn a chore into a pleasure while diminishing the chance of errors in the process.

Whether you're a novice or an expert, keep in mind that you're the one who establishes a tool's real value. The best tools don't always make the best woodworker—if used poorly, even expensive items can be close to useless. When purchasing new tools, invest in the best ones you can afford. But keep in mind that a good woodworker can work miracles with modest tools.

If you buy new power tools, don't discard the instructional pamphlets that come with them. Sometimes they include tips that could come in handy once you've put in a few hours of practice, preferably on some pieces of scrap wood. Beyond that, there are some excellent books available to guide novice and accomplished woodworkers through various techniques specific to individual tools.

WORKBENCH

A sturdy workbench is essential to any woodworking project, particularly in doormaking, which requires a larger-than-usual platform as well. A workbench provides a level surface where you can measure, clamp, glue, drill, and chisel—and it can be a storage place besides if there's a shelf underneath.

One feature of a good workbench is its stability; the heavier it is, the less likely it will be to shift as you work. You can lessen any risk of movement by placing the bench against a solid wall, but then you lose the ability to walk all the way around it, which can be a plus if your shop is large enough.

Another detail especially important to door-building is a level top. A warped surface can easily translate to a warped door. A solid-core door itself can be and often is used as a top. If you can't buy a large, sturdy, level bench, the best approach is to build one; detailed instructions and a list of materials is included on page 16.

Workbenches of high quality will include a vise, a tool well, dogs (steel or wooden pegs slipped into holes in the top and used as backstops in wide-clamping), and solid stretchers between the legs for extra support. For comfort and working ease, try to set the top at 34" or close to hip height.

A door bench is convenient but not all that necessary to someone just building a few doors. It's a stand that holds a door securely on edge for planing and marking. If you were installing a number of doors on a regular basis, the door bench would be worth building. Details and materials are listed on page 17.

Measuring tools come in a variety of shapes and sizes.

MEASURING AND MARKING TOOLS

Measuring and marking are the basis to successful carpentry. No other stage of the construction process has as much influence on the finished product as does the laying out of lengths, joints, and angles. Correctly marked and measured dimensions are critical, so don't underestimate the importance of these detail tools.

Measuring tools establish length, width, and depth. They're useful when you purchase raw stock (it's always wise to check the lumber's actual dimensions before you buy it), and they're absolutely necessary when you're building a woodworking project.

Marking tools are helpful in locating the lines, points, curves, and angles where you intend to cut, rout, plane, or drill.

STEEL TAPE MEASURE

Steel tapes are long rulers that roll up into a compact case. They're made in widths between 1/4" and 1" and in lengths from 6' to 25'or more. The tape end has a hook that secures to one end of the work; this should be loosely mounted to compensate for the width of the hook in both inside and outside measurements.

A large, solid workbench made from standard commercial lumber.

Graduations are noted in 1/16" increments (except for the first 12", which are marked in 1/32" increments). For door-building projects, a 3/4"-wide, 16'-long, self-retracting rule with a tape-lock button would be the best choice.

STRAIGHTEDGE

A straightedge—called a steel rule when marked with graduations—comes in handy for drawing straight lines. It's a steel or aluminum ruler, 12" to 36" long, which can be used for fine measuring and marking when graduated.

TRY SQUARE

This small (5-1/2" x 8") square is used to check right angles; a ruler along the edge of its blade can be used to take quick measurements.

The combination square and the try square are used for close marking.

COMBINATION SQUARE

The adjustable combination square is a 4-1/2" X 12" tool with a sliding blade and a 45-degree shoulder built right into the stock. The blade can be locked at any point and its end used as a marking point for a pencil.

FRAMING SQUARE

A framing square is shaped like a large right angle and is used to check for 90-degree accuracy on a large scale. Its two edges are 16" x 24" long and are marked with ruler graduations in 1/8" and 1/16" increments. The framing square is used mainly in construc-

tion carpentry, but its size makes it handy for spot-checking the larger door projects.

MARKING GAUGE

A marking gauge is used to scribe a line at a point in relation to an edge. Its hardwood stock holds a graduated inch-scale beam that slides through its center. The beam is locked in position with a thumbscrew, and a steel spur at the end marks the wood when the gauge is pushed along the work.

COMPASS

A compass has a pivot at the top and two legs, one with a pointed end and one with a pencil tip. This tool is used to scribe and transfer radius arcs, circles, and patterns during the layout process.

PROTRACTOR

A woodworker's protractor is a simple tool used to determine angles. It has a head with a flat base, upon which a pivoting blade is attached. The blade is aligned with the angle, which is then indicated in degrees on a graduated scale etched into the head.

LEVEL

A level is used to establish whether a framing member is level (if it's horizontal) or plumb (if it's vertical). It uses a bubble captured within a small tube of viscous liquid to determine the degree off "center" the object in question may be. A long, thin frame of aluminum or wood houses three bubble vials, two at the end positioned to read for plumb, and one in the center set to read for level. For door work, a framing level at least 48" in length is best.

PLUMB BOB

This tool is simply an 8-ounce weight with a sharp point connected to a nylon line. When suspended from an overhead point, it's used to transfer that point's position to the ground or a framing member below.

PLANING TOOLS

Planes are used to bring down the thickness or width of wood stock to a uniform level. In doormaking especially, much of the better wood you purchase—especially if it's not a common commercial species—will be rough-cut or surfaced (planed) on one or two sides only. It's up to you to custom-size your stock unless you contract with a millwork shop to do it for you.

BENCH PLANE

This is a hand-held tool with a blade set at an angle within a steel frame. The edge of the blade is adjusted to protrude slightly from a slot in the sole, or base, of the body. The variety of hand planes, and the jobs they do, is enormous—but for general shop work, a plane with a 1-3/4" to 2" blade and a sole 9" to 10" long is ideal.

Other planes may be mentioned in the instructions for the individual projects. A jack plane is a large tool, usually with a 2" blade and a 14" sole, used to make very accurate, consistent cuts. A block plane is a small, hand-sized plane with, give or take a few fractions, a 2" X 6" body used for local work.

POWER PLANE

This is a hand-held power tool made to plane large amounts of stock from a board's surface rapidly. A typical power plane has a two-edged rotary blade about 3-1/4" wide and a sole between 10" and 12" long. Depending on its horsepower and the speed of its rotary cutter, a power plane can remove from 1/32" to 1/16" of wood in each pass.

The block plane is a one-hand planing tool.

THICKNESS PLANER

A stationary tool used to plane rough-cut boards to a uniform thickness. A portable or "benchtop" planer is relatively inexpensive and can handle boards up to 12" wide and 6" thick, removing a maximum of 1/16" of material with each pass.

A larger standing stationary planer can be three to six times more costly and accommodate a board up to 20" wide and 8" thick. Higher-amperage or 220-volt service might be needed for these larger tools.

JOINTER

A stationary tool designed to put a consistent and accurate edge on a board in preparation for making a joint. Though a saw blade can make a reasonably accurate cut, kerf marks and variances in the movement of the blade make a cut edge too inconsistent for fine results.

Benchtop jointers are manufactured, but most are stand-mounted and built to handle boards 6" to 8" wide. A large fence designed to tilt right and left, 45 degrees each direction, allows the cutting of beveled edges. The better jointers have a 1/2" depth of cut and the capability to complete a 1/2" rabbet.

CLAMPING TOOLS

Clamps are used to hold parts to each other or to a bench so that you can mark, drill, or cut them, and they also serve to hold glued parts together as the glue dries. Used with strips of wood, clamps can be made into saw and router guides or extended to clamp over an enlarged area.

C-CLAMPS

C-clamps derive their name from the basic "C" shape of their steel or iron frames. One end of the "C" (the anvil) is fixed; it doesn't move at all. The other end is fitted with a threaded rod and swivel pad. When the threaded end is tightened, whatever is between it and the fixed end is tightly gripped. Pads or scraps of wood should be used between the jaws and your work so that the work isn't marred when the clamp is tightened.

C-clamps come in a variety of styles and sizes, but in general they're small; woodworking C-clamps are usually limited to a 12" jaw opening, but for the projects in this book a 4" or 6" size is fine.

BAR AND PIPE CLAMPS

These clamps are made to span long or wide pieces of wood frame, panels, or doors, or to grip several pieces of wood

Pipe clamps, bar clamps, and C-clamps are all used in making doors.

that are placed edge-to-edge. Their frames are simply steel or aluminum bars, or sections of iron plumbing pipe that are several feet in length. At one end is a fixed head, equipped with a short, threaded rod and a metal pad. At the other end is a sliding tail-stop that can be locked in any position along the bar or pipe to accommodate the work.

Pipe clamps are less expensive than (but not quite as effective as) bar clamps but can be made 6' or more in length. To reduce expenses you can buy pipe clamp kits, which include only the fixtures; purchase the pipe itself—and have its end threaded—at a local plumbing supply store. For the door projects, six 48"-long, 3/4" pipe clamps should suffice.

VISES

A vise is just a bench-mounted clamp. It can be used to hold work pieces together or to hold stock securely while you work on it. A woodworker's vise has smooth, broad jaws that are usually drilled so that facings can be installed to prevent marring fine work. Better wood vises include a dog; this is a bar that slides up from the vise's movable jaw to hold work against a similar stop mounted on the bench itself. The dog extends the vise's effective jaw opening by 24" or more. Some vises also make use of a half-nut to provide quick-slide opening and closing; tightening occurs only once the work is in place.

A stationary jointer can surface and edge a board to perfection.

CUTTING TOOLS

A saw's function is determined by the number, pitch, bevel, and angle of teeth on its blade. The higher the number of teeth per inch of blade (a measurement given in "points"), the smoother the blade's cut will be. A saw with fewer points will make a coarser cut, but it will also cut more quickly. A backsaw, for instance, with 15 teeth per inch, is used for fine joinery work; a crosscut saw, with perhaps 8 teeth per inch, can make rapid cuts across thick lumber.

Though most of these door projects could be made with hand tools, it's more realistic to assume that most of your cutting will be done with power saws, and you'll certainly have an easier job of it. Power saws often use what are

Even a small miter box is adequate for most door work.

A circular saw can be used to handle many rough-cutting jobs.

known as combination blades, which offer clean cuts both with and against the wood's grain.

CROSSCUT SAW

As its name suggests, a crosscut saw is used to cut across or against the wood's grain. Though crosscut saw lengths vary, a 26" version will work well for any hand-sawing you do, except through plywood. Crosscut saws are available with 7 through 12 points per inch, depending on how coarse or fine you wish the cut to be. Remember, the greater the number, the smoother the cut—and the more slowly it's made.

RIPSAW

A ripsaw is designed to cut with or along the wood's grain. Most ripsaws are 26" long and come with 4-1/2 through 7 points per inch. If you have no power saws and plenty of ambition, you'll want to own both a ripcut and a crosscut saw. While it is possible to rip with a crosscut saw, you can't make a clean cross cut with a ripsaw.

COPING SAW

The steel-bow frame of a coping saw is "U" shaped. A very thin blade, with 10 to 12 teeth per inch, is mounted between the tips of the U. This saw is especially useful for cutting curves because its frame can be angled away from the line of cut. It is designed to do well on boards thicker than 3/4".

BACKSAW

A fine-toothed hand saw used in joinery to make smooth, accurate cuts. The steel back frame fastened to the upper edge of the blade stiffens it and gives the saw its name.

MITER BOX

A frame used in conjunction with a backsaw to hand-cut miters in boards and trim. Specially designed compound miter boxes allow beveled miter cuts as well.

CIRCULAR SAW

The motor-driven, hand-held circular saw is one of the most popular power tools around. The standard version has a 7-1/4" blade that can be adjusted to cut at angles between 90 degrees and 45 degrees. When set to cut at a perpendicular, blade penetration is 2-1/4"; at 45 degrees, it's reduced to 1-3/4". The greatest disadvantage to a circular saw is that it's heavy and can be unwieldy, which affects its accuracy.

Better-quality circular saws are usually equipped with a carbide-tipped combination blade, but regular blades will do just as well if you sharpen or replace them regularly. A good blade can be installed on an inexpensive saw to improve its performance.

COMPOUND MITER SAW

Sometimes called a chop saw or cutoff saw, this is a portable power tool that's evolved through several stages. The least expensive version is similar to a circular saw but mounted on a short table with a pivoting hinge. It pulls down to cut, and can be swung right and left 45 degrees to cut miters. The next type includes a beveling feature that lets the blade tilt as well, allowing a compound bevel cut. The ultimate model uses a slide mount so the blade and motor can be pulled down and forward up to 12" in the manner of a radial arm saw and can cut miters and bevels as well. Blade diameters range from 8-1/2" to 12".

RADIAL ARM SAW

A stationary tool used to cross-cut long pieces of stock on a large fixed table. It uses a powerful motor and 10" blade suspended on a carriage from a beam that can be swung right and left and raised and lowered as well. The blade can also be tilted to make bevel cuts. A pivot in the carriage allows the motor and blade to be turned 90 degrees for making rip cuts, but that procedure doesn't yield the best results with this kind of saw.

TABLE SAW AND DADO BLADE

The table saw uses a powerful motor built into a frame and table. Its weight and design will give a more accurate cut than a hand-held circular saw can deliver. The typical table saw has a pivoting carriage that holds the blade's arbor, or axle. This construction allows the blade to be raised to a 90-degree cutting depth of 3-1/8"—and tilted up to 45 degrees, which gives a 2-1/8" cut at that angle.

Generally, table saws are equipped with a 10" carbide-tipped combination blade. Compact and portable table saws that use smaller blades, but that have the same features as the larger models, are also available.

Table saws come with a rip fence, a long, straight bar that runs parallel to the exposed blade and can be adjusted to either side of it. The fence assures accurate rip cuts by guiding material into the blade.

A miter gauge, which is adjustable to 45 degrees on either side of its 90-degree midpoint, helps in making miter cuts by holding the stock at the correct angle as it's passed through the blade.

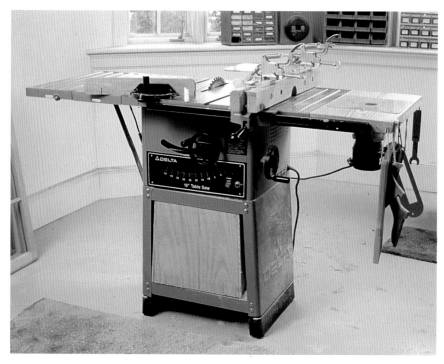

A well-equipped table saw, with extensions, set up on site during remodeling.

A dado blade is a specially designed cutting tool that's fitted to a table saw to make wide grooves and notches. There are two common dado designs. One uses an offset blade that wobbles to the right and to the left as it revolves. The other design uses two outer blades and a number of inner "chippers" that are stacked to establish the exact width of the cut.

JIGSAW

The hand-held jigsaw, or its variant the sabre saw, is the powered alternative to a coping saw and is used to cut curves, free-form shapes, and large holes in panels or boards up to 1-1/2" thick. Cutting action is provided by a narrow, reciprocating bayonet-style blade that moves very rapidly. A shoe surrounding the blade can be tilted 45 degrees to the right and left of perpendicular for angled cuts.

The best jigsaws have a variable speed control and an orbital blade action; this action swings the cutting edge forward into the work and back again, through the blade's up-and-down cycle. A dust blower keeps the cut clear, and the tool may also come with a circle-cutting guide and rip fence as well.

A jigsaw's thin, narrow blade can be maneuvered around corners.

The teeth of a dado blade remove wood to create a slot in a hurry.

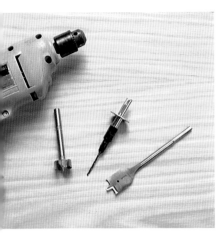

An electric drill and spade, screw, and Forstner specialty bits.

Screw bits are specially-sized to fit the various diameter wood screws.

UTILITY KNIFE

This inexpensive tool can be used to cut thin wood and material and to scribe lines for marking. The best kinds have retractable blades and a blade storage pocket in the handle.

DRILLING AND BORING TOOLS

Cutting clean holes through wood requires the use of drills and bits suited for the job. Holes can be functional, decorative, or designed with special features such as a tapered countersink opening or an internal shoulder.

3/8" VARIABLE SPEED REVERSIBLE DRILL

Though you can bore almost any hole with a hand-operated drill, there's little reason not to own this versatile tool, which operates more quickly and with less effort than any hand-operated drill. For most any project, a drill with a 3/8" chuck capacity and a motor amperage of 3.5 amps or greater will do just fine. Cordless versions are made and are appropriate for driving screws and drilling small holes, but they may not be suitable for continuous, heavy-duty work.

At a small extra cost, you can get an electric drill with a variable speed control. This feature allows you to govern the speed of the drill's motor by simply varying the pressure you exert on a the tool's trigger. A reversible motor is included with this option, which permits you to take screws out just as quickly as you insert them.

STOP COLLARS

When you need to control the depth of a drill bit's penetration, use a stop collar. These are metal (or sometimes plastic) rings that tighten onto the drill bit's shaft. When the bit sinks into the wood, the collar hits the wood's face and stops the bit from going any deeper. Stop collars are sized to different drill bit diameters.

COUNTERSINKS

A project's appearance and function can suffer when the head of a screw protrudes above the face of the wood. In order to hide these heads, a countersink is used. These angle-faced bits cut shallow, slope-sided holes into the surface of the work, creating a recess into which the screw's head rests, flush with the face of the work.

SPECIALTY BITS

A variety of drill bits are made to accomplish specific tasks. Forstner bits are used to drill clean, flat-bottomed holes when a fine cut is called for. They are made in 1/4" to 2-1/4" diameters. Spade bits (used with power drills) bore quickly and make rough but effective holes through wood. They're designed with a center point and two flat cutting edges and come in 1/4" to 1-1/2" diameters.

Screw bits are countersink/pilot drills that combine the hole-drilling and countersinking processes in one operation. The better versions of these bits use what's known as a tapered bit, which follows the contour of a standard wood screw; they also include a stop collar. These combination bits are made for screw size Nos. 5 through 12. This type of drill bit is particularly versatile because it allows the woodworker to countersink a fastener flush with the wood's surface or to counterbore the hole to give the screw a deeper penetration where desirable.

Extension bits, and extension shafts made to fit spade and other types of power bits, allow you to bore hole deeper than a normal-length bit would allow. The extra-length bits come in diameters from 3/16" to 3/4" and usually are 18" long; the spade bit extension shafts come in 18" and 24" lengths and are made to fit standard 5/16" and 7/16" power bit shanks.

CHISELING AND ROUTING TOOLS

Joinery and decorative work both rely on tools that are able to make sharp, detailed cuts, or create consistent shapes along an edge of or within a piece of wood. Regardless of whether these tools are hand- or machine-operated, they use a sharp cutting edge to do their work.

CHISELS

One type of chisel is all that's necessary for these door projects—the standard mortise chisel. This cabinetmaker's tool is used to clean up joints and mortises, shave glue and grain from a joint, or simply remove layers of wood cleanly from one spot. A set of four or five bevel-edge chisels for hand or mallet work, in sizes from 1/4" to 1" wide and 7" to 10" long, would be sufficient. Occasionally you may need to work them with a mallet, though hand-shaving is easy enough if the blade is sharp. The best types are reinforced to prevent the handles from splitting with use.

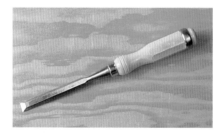

A 1/2" chisel is an often-used manual woodworking tool.

ROUTERS

A router's job is to cut grooves and rabbets, shape edges, and make slots, and it does that work easily and quickly. You'll find that doors often include framing members with rounded or chamfered edges. These can be cut with a router and a roundover or chamfer bit. Similar edges can be cut with gouges, rasps, and sanders, but it takes some time and often results in some visible inconsistencies.

Router bits are held in a collet on the end of a shaft, which in turn is support-

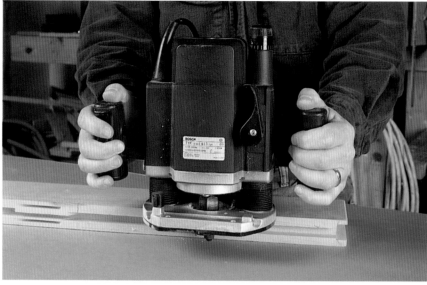

ed by a flat base and housing. The shape of the bit determines what type of cut will be made in the work, and handles on the housing allow the operator to control the direction of the bit. The simplest routers have 3/8" collets, external clamp-depth controls, and 6-amp motors. More sophisticated models are known as plunge routers; these allow vertical entry into the work for precise cutting and have 1/2" collets, variable-speed 12- to 15- amp motors, and variable depth controls.

In a well-equipped workshop, routing work is done on a router table, which is just a stand with a cast surface that uses a heavy-duty 1/2" router inverted and mounted from the bottom. An adjustable fence and a special see-through guard allow you to guide the work through the exposed bit safely.

A shaper is a stationary routing tool that uses a powerful motor and a 1/2" or 3/4" spindle to handle work beyond the capability of a table-mounted router—such as moldings, heavy raised panels, and hardwood trim.

ROUTER BITS

The design and shape of a router bit dictates what form the finished edge or groove will take. There are over 200 router-bit styles available for various types of work, though for the projects

A plunge router on the job, cutting a slot.

The shaper cuts a definite profile into a piece of wood.

A selection of router bits, used to cut edges or slots.

in this book only a few are needed. When cutting or shaping an edge, a router bit with a ball-bearing pilot at its tip is used. The tip rolls along the edge below the part of the wood being cut, assuring a high degree of accuracy.

Groove- or slot-cutting bits cannot use pilot tips, so a guide or temporary fence is often used when routing a channel. This guide is a device that clamps onto the base of the tool and acts as a moving fence to keep the router and bit following the edge of the work.

Either type of bit is set vertically by adjusting the router base to control the depth of cut.

JOINING TOOLS

Once boards and components are prepared for joining, several tools can be used to complete the joint. Small backsaws and chisels are the traditional means to this end, but newer methods have also developed in the interest of saving time.

DOWELING JIG
This is a precision frame used to center holes on the edge of a board up to about 2" thick. Various-sized holes correspond to the diameter of the dowels being used, and the jig allows these holes to be placed exactly on the mating pieces, so the edges of the joined boards are aligned both vertically and horizontally. It's used mainly for edge-joining and certain framing applications.

BISCUIT JOINERS
The first biscuit, or plate, joiner was designed for production work over 40 years ago. Over the past decade, many manufacturers have developed small, inexpensive versions for the home woodworker. It's just a high-speed rotary saw with a blade about 4-1/8" in diameter and 4mm thick. The cutter is set on a vertical axis so it cuts horizontally as it plunges into the edge of the work. An adjustable miter fence permits joinery on square and beveled edges, and a depth adjuster sets the plunge level to correspond with the size of biscuit to be used. There are three different sizes of biscuits (Nos. 0, 10, and 20) that range in length from 2-1/8" to 2-9/16" and in width from 1-1/8" to 1-7/8".

SANDING AND SMOOTHING TOOLS

To properly finish a piece of wood, it's often necessary to level surfaces by removing material and to smooth the grain. Files and rasps cut or round edges and small areas; sandpaper prepares the wood for its final finish.

A palm sander can save considerable time if used properly.

SANDERS AND SANDPAPER
Sanding can be done by hand or with power sanders. If you choose to sand by hand, you'll want to purchase a hand-sanding block. It's a small, palm-held, hard rubber tool with a flat surface at the bottom and a clip mechanism at each end to keep the sandpaper tightly in place.

The hand-held orbital finishing sander—called a palm or pad sander—has a palm grip and either a round or square pad to which sandpaper is attached. The orbiting mechanism requires at least a 1-1/2- or 2-amp motor to be effective. For convenience, the round styles use self-adhesive paper on the pad rather than mechanical clips.

Sandpaper and the replaceable pads for palm sanders come in a variety of grits (or degrees of roughness): coarse (No. 60), medium (No. 80), fine (No. 150),

The biscuit joiner cuts precision slots to accommodate wooden plates used in modern joinery.

and very-fine (No. 220). Other grits in between are also manufactured. Standard garnet paper is suitable for woodwork and is unique in that the abrasive particles continuously break away, exposing fresh material as they do; aluminum-oxide sanding sheets, however, are more durable and less likely to clog up with particles.

RASPS AND FILES

Wood rasps are coarse-cutting hand tools used to make the first cut in removing wood stock for shaping or rounding. A finer cabinet rasp is made for second-cut work. Rasps come in three styles: flat on both sides, half-round on one side, and round. Wood files are less coarse than rasps and are used for finer smoothing and finishing work. Like rasps, they're about 10" long; they usually come in round and half-round cross sections. For the projects in this book, only a flat rasp might be needed. But in general, two grades of files are good to have on hand. These are a 10" or 12" bastard-cut file, one step finer than a coarse file and with a half-round back that allows it to be used on inside curves and arcs; For finish work, a smooth-cut file, which is the least coarse of the group and especially suited to hardwoods.

DUST COLLECTORS

Sawdust can be an irritant and even a health hazard over time. Even ten or fifteen minutes' exposure to fine wood dust can cause discomfort and affect breathing for days afterward. A dust mask or respirator will filter material, but a shop dust collector will remove sawdust at the source and contain it in a canister for later disposal. A moderate investment will allow you to move air at 500 or 600 cubic feet per minute through a 4" tube from a single source such as a table saw or router table. Larger machines with up to 2,000-cfm capacity can collect from several tools at once.

HAMMERING AND SETTING TOOLS

HAMMERS

The hammer you're most likely to use in finishing work is a lightweight tack hammer, 3-1/2 or 6 ounces in weight. A claw style will do, but even better is a Warrington hammer because it has one traditional flat face and one elongated peen for starting the small brads used to set trim.

NAILSET

A nailset is simply a fine-pointed punch used to set the head of a finishing nail or brad below the surface of the wood without enlarging the nail hole.

MALLETS

If you need a larger hammer for chisel work or setting joints, an 8" wooden carpenter's mallet of 12 ounces or so would do well. Plastic-headed mallets are also used for this type of work.

A hammer and a nailset, for driving and sinking finishing nails beneath the wood's surface.

SCREWDRIVING TOOLS

The screw fasteners called for in the majority of the door projects use a No. 2 Phillips head, which assures a positive, nearly slipless grip. Larger Phillips-head screws (No. 12 and up) are driven with a No. 3 Phillips screwdriver tip. More traditional slotted screws can be used as a substitute anywhere you wish, but be warned that flat-bladed screwdrivers are more inclined to slip and mar your work, especially in the hands of a novice.

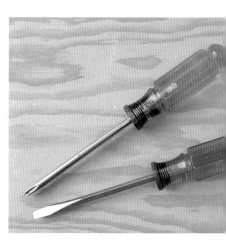

Two screwdrivers, a flat-blade type and the more positive-grip Phillips design.

SCREWDRIVERS

A screwdriver can come with a variety of tips, but a 6" or 8" No. 2 Phillips driver with a molded or wooden handle is the one to use on the No. 6, No. 8, and No. 10 Phillips head screws usually used in this book's projects.

POWER DRIVERS

Most woodworkers use power-drive bits in combination with cabinet, dry-wall, or deck screws to save time. These bits—used with hand-held drivers or 3/8" variable-speed power drills—have a short, six-sided shank that slips easily into the drill chuck. The tip can be a Phillips or straight-bladed design, though a square-drive tip to fit matching screws is a popular option.

CHAPTER 5

GLUES AND FASTENERS

FASTENERS

For the purpose of definition, fasteners are the metal hardware that holds things together. This would include screws, lag bolts, brads, and nails, but technically not wooden items that do much the same job, such as dowels and biscuits (these are considered elements of joinery).

Fortunately, doormaking and installation largely rely on only a few types of fasteners. Flathead Phillips drive screws are used, as are the newer variations of this traditional tapered fastener, the bugle-head drywall or cabinet screw. The old-style slotted flathead screw may be appropriate for a special application or to match a period look, but they're generally difficult to work with because they really should be countersunk and hand-driven, which takes time many do not wish to expend.

Screws are sized by gauge number, which indicates their diameter at the body or shank, directly beneath the head. They're also made in graduated lengths, up to 6" in some cases. So, a 5/32"-diameter screw 2" long is sold as a No. 8 X 2" screw. Refer to the accompanying chart for standard screw dimensions.

Besides the drive design and the shape of the head, the finish on a screw and the material it's made from come into play. Cadmium- or zinc-plated steel is

the minimum general-use screw. A chrome- or nickel-plated steel screw is used to present a lasting appearance when exposed to the weather. Solid brass screws are expensive—and lack the strength of steel—but stand up to weather beautifully.

The term "deck screw" is mentioned occasionally. This type of steel screw fastener has a special coating—either galvanized, anodized, or silicone-bronzed—that makes it especially weather-resistant, which is ideal for any outdoor application.

Lag screws are large-diameter square- or hexagonal-head steel fasteners with shank sizes ranging from 1/4" to 1/2" and lengths from 1" to 8", broken down in 1/2" increments. They're used for the sake of appearance and for applications in which screws larger than No. 12 are needed. Machine screws—which include steel carriage bolts and anything else that uses a nut to secure a part—are more substantial than wood screws, and are more positive because the washer and nut prevent pullout on a stressed part.

Brads, or wire nails, are used for strips and trim. Their diameters are indicated by wire gauge (19g through 12g), the higher number expressing a thinner nail. A 16-gauge brad is .065" in diameter, an 18-gauge .049". Lengths vary

Wood screws come in a variety of styles, but the flathead cabinet type is a modern standard.

from 1/4" to 1-1/2". Being small, brads are used to secure strips which aren't under a lot of stress. Other nails are used for more substantial construction, and their diameters are measured in penny sizes, indicated by the letter "d". (Penny sizing originated in England many years ago when nails were sold for so many pennies per hundred.) All nails of a particular penny size are the same length, but diameters vary from one type of nail to another. Penny sizes range from 2d (1") to 60d (6") in length.

Common nails have flat heads and hold framing members together. Casing or finish nails have set heads—designed to penetrate slightly below the surface of the wood for later filling—and are used for casing and trim pieces. In general, the thinner finish nails are made in sizes up to 10d (finish) or 16d (casing). Concrete or masonry nails are hardened steel, up to 3" long, and some have fluted shanks to aid in penetration.

■ SCREW CHART ■

Size or gauge No.	4	6	8	10	12
Shank diameter	7/64"	9/64"	5/32"	3/16"	7/32"
Lengths (by 1/4s)	3/8"-1"	1/2"-2"	1/2"-3"	3/4"-3-1/2"	3/4"-3-1/2"
Shank hole drill	1/8"	9/64"	11/64"	3/16"	7/32"
Pilot hole drill	1/16"	5/64"	3/32"	7/64"	1/8"

A one-part aliphatic resin is an excellent woodworking glue for doors.

GLUES AND ADHESIVES

The most reasonably priced general-purpose wood glue for piece-built doors is a nontoxic Type II (above waterline) one-part waterproof wood glue. The precatalyzed aliphatic resin currently on the market offers the advantages of regular yellow carpenter's glue (10-minute setting, 12- to 24-hour curing) but resists the effects of water and weather.

If this type of adhesive isn't available, a more costly one-part moisture-curing urethane glue has recently been developed that is both flexible and quite versatile. This glue is nontoxic and has a short "in-clamp" time of 1 to 4 hours, with a slightly longer curing time. Urethane is stronger than aliphatic glues and is not thermoplastic, which means that it won't migrate from cured joints as a result of humidity or temperature fluctuations. It can also be used on wood that has a higher moisture content than kiln dried stock.

A possible third type of adhesive is a two-part resorcinol, which takes about 12 hours to set and at least another 12 to cure completely. This is a costly boat builder's glue that would not be used except under extreme circumstances.

For best results, the material to be glued should be clean, dry, and free of any oils. Slightly rough—but not gapped—surfaces make the best bond. Any glue should be wiped immediately from the outside surface of the wood with a damp cloth if it runs from the joint, or it'll make the wood difficult to sand and finish later on.

Decorative studs and wrought-iron grill-work in the light frames make this eight-panel apartment door distinctive—along with faux strap hinges mounted to the lock stile (the lockset has been repositioned).

CHAPTER 6

SANDING AND SURFACE PREPARATION

The proper sanding rate and the right paper can make a huge difference in the quality of your preparation work.

ONE OF THE MOST COMMON mistakes inexperienced woodworkers make is in rushing through quite possibly the most unpleasant part of the whole wood-shop game—sanding. That may be understandable, given the circumstances…but what's not is the fact that most probably aren't doing it on purpose. They just don't realize that they're moving too fast, and a poor finish is all they've got to show for it.

A finish is only as good as the surface beneath it, and getting that surface just right takes a lot of time and a little bit of know-how. Later on in Chapters 9 and 10, you'll see how the selection and preparation of your stock factors in to the doormaking process—but now, this overview on sanding and surface prep should satisfy the novices and offer a little review material for the experienced.

Before you begin to think about sanding, you should take a good look at the wood you're about to work with. If you had it surfaced (or planed and jointed it yourself) and handled it carefully in working, there should be little problem. But sight down it in good light anyway. The wood should be flat and the surface smooth before any coating is applied. Any glue runs or forceout should have been cleaned off with a damp cloth before it dried.

If there is a dent in the wood large enough to notice or bother with, it can be removed with water and an ordinary clothes iron. Set the door on a horizontal surface and place a drop or two of water in the depression. Let it sit for a moment to give the fibers a chance to absorb it, then cover the spot with a damp cloth and touch the tip of a hot iron to it—no longer than two or three seconds at the most. The heat will cause the steam to expand rapidly,

popping out the compressed wood-fiber cell walls as it rises. The impression should become level after one or two trys. If not, the grain has probably been shredded, and the gouge will need to be filled.

You should know, too, that some manufactured wood pieces—moldings and millwork in particular—may have been contaminated with silicone oils or waxes left there as cutter-head lubricants. These should be removed with a coarse cloth soaked in mineral spirits, followed by an ammonia wash of one part clear ammonia to fifteen parts warm water, spread evenly over the entire surface, then wiped dry. Waxes and oils are generally compatible with oil-based finishes but can mottle water-based finishes and lacquers; they must be removed before proceeding.

Coated abrasive is the technical term for sandpaper, which is nothing more than tiny pieces of mineral grit glued onto a backing of some kind. The grit determines how fast a paper will sand and how much effort will be required to do it. The backing—and the glue or "binder" used to hold the grit in place—establishes how the sheet will stand up to wear and solvents.

There's not a whole lot to understanding how sandpaper works. The abrasive removes tool marks left in the surface of the wood and replaces them with grooves established by the size of the grit on the paper. Relatively few large grooves are turned into many small grooves as a progressively finer grit size is used.

The terms "open coat" and "closed coat" are used to describe the amount of grit on the backing. An open coat has only about 50% to 70% of the surface covered with mineral. This has the effect of periodically declogging the paper, because the open spaces provide a place for the cuttings to lodge until they fall off. A closed coat is completely covered with sand, which offers a finer finish. In higher-grit (extra-fine) papers, the difference doesn't amount to much because the rough work has already, in theory, been done. But with the lower-numbered grits, the open-style paper generates less heat and conserves material.

Grits can be either synthetic or natural. Though there are many different kinds of sandpaper, only a few are really practical for woodworking. Among the synthetic grits, aluminum oxide is the most common and probably the one you'll use. It's light brown or white in color and is ideal for general sanding and finishing work. For finishing specifically, another synthetic—silicon carbide, which is bright black in appearance—is often recommended.

Garnet is a reddish mineral used extensively in sandpaper, even with the advent of synthetics. It has the unique characteristic of breaking off as it works, presenting a new sharp facet with each fracture. Garnet paper does an excellent job but wears faster than the synthetics.

The backing used with sandpapers varies according to the tool the paper is going to be used on. Sheet papers are designated by the letters A, C, D, E, F according to thickness, light to heavy. For belts and discs, polyester cloth backings, labeled by thickness from J to X,Y, and T, are used. Practically speaking, your backing choices will probably be limited, and you'll end up using what's available. For hand-held palm sanders, a backing with pressure-sensitive adhesive is becoming increasingly common.

When sanding, always work from coarse to fine grits. You should begin with an 80 or 100 grit, and then progress to the next finer level, increasing the point range with each step.

Using this rule, a grit progression of 80/120/220/400 would be typical.

Working with too heavy a grit size results in a lot of effort with no progress, because you're simply creating grooves. Conversely, using too light a grit doesn't remove the deeper marks from the previous paper, so they'll eventually show up in the finish. Surprisingly enough, many woods don't require you to sand finer than 180 grit. The harder woods, however, may need to be descratched to a 400-grit or higher level. In general, a 220-grit sanding will give the best results, especially if you plan on using a water-based finish.

Besides the motor-driven palm sander, you may be using a sanding block to assure a flat surface and get a better feel for your work. You can also double- or triple-fold a paper sheet to do detail work or stiffen the paper in your fingers. Once you reach a 150-grit or finer level, you can begin sanding in any direction—not just with the grain—because the scratches you create will not likely be visible.

The most common error people make when using a palm sander is scrubbing it across the wood's surface too rapidly. Keep in mind that an oscillating sander is already moving (at a rate between 10,000 and 14,000 oscillations per minute) and you don't need to speed it up. Your hand with the sander in it should move about one inch per second to avoid leaving swirl marks in the surface.

■ GRIT CHART ■

Grade No.	Coarseness Rating
600	Super fine
500	
400	
360	Extra fine
320	
280	
240	Very fine
220	
180	
150	Fine
120	
100	
80	Medium
60	
50	
40	Coarse

CHAPTER 7

CHOOSING AND USING FINISHES

A DOOR'S WOODEN SURFACE is exposed to all sorts of stress and abuse. Sunlight, weather, dirty hands, and sharp claws all take their toll on a finish, and can eliminate altogether certain coatings that would never stand up to a door's hard lot in life.

Realistically, only a few finishes are suitable for doors, and the requirements are simple—they need to be durable and easy to maintain. This pretty much eliminates lacquer paints and oil finishes, which just don't provide enough protection. But good old-fashioned varnish and gloss enamel paint are naturals, and certain kinds of synthetics like polyurethane are worth considering as well.

A finish has several functions. It protects the wood from stains and wear, preserves it from the effects of sunlight and moisture, enhances it to bring out color and grain patterns, and can even alter it by covering defects or adding color. It does all these things by covering the wood with a thin film of resin, made fluid by the addition of a solvent that evaporates during drying.

If you do even a bit of research on finishes, you'll soon come across the terms "evaporative" and "reactive" to describe the two categories of finishes. The difference can be explained without going into deep chemical explanations simply by saying that evaporative finishes start as a flowable resin and dry as a hardened resin. Nothing changes other than the fact that the solvent has evaporated. Reactive finishes, on the other hand, undergo a chemical change as the film

Quarter-sawn oak and full-beveled panels contribute to the already distinctive look of this English cottage door with its tapered center rail, stained-glass lights, and functional rim lock.

is formed to become an entirely different material.

From a practical standpoint, the distinction means two things. First, evaporative finishes can be re-dissolved once they've dried by introducing the original solvent. This happens in essence every time a new coat is applied, and when everything is said and done, the finished film is one single layer. This is not true of a reactive finish, which dries in stacks as separate layers. Second, evaporative finishes, because of the characteristic just described, are a lot easier to maintain when necessary because repairs on them generally don't show. Probably the only evaporative finish you'd consider for a door is a water-based polyurethane varnish, simply called a polyurethane coating.

Of the reactives, polyurethane varnish in an oil base offers all the good characteristics of hardness, adhesion, water resistance, flexibility, and abrasion resistance. However, polyurethane is not particularly resistant to ultraviolet radiation and isn't recommended for surfaces exposed to direct sunlight. On the other hand, it can be applied over stains and existing finishes, so it remains a popular choice.

Spar varnish is excellent for outdoor use, for—true to its name—it works well on wood exposed to the weather. It is an oil-based synthetic resin that's very flexible and can also stand up to ultraviolet radiation. It adheres well to wood and can go over stains and most other finishes.

Enamel paint has the advantage of providing a smooth, hard, colorful finish that fends off moisture and protects the wood from abrasion and the effects of direct sunlight. For a door with a number of architectural elements, the way paint is applied can highlight certain features and mute others. Decorative designs can also be painted right on an ordinary door's surface (see the sidebar on page 43) to make it an extraordinary—and functional—work of art.

In softwoods or wood that has a tendency to absorb a finish, a sanding sealer should be used to prepare the wood before applying paint or stain. Usually, a single coat will be sufficient, and giving the wood a light sanding after it's applied will bring down any raised grain. If you plan on staining the wood to bring out its natural characteristics, you'll have to do that before applying the protective finish.

For some exterior applications, you might consider a semitransparent stain to enhance the natural colors of the base wood and provide weather protection—as long as you don't mind periodic maintenance. These stains soak into the wood and repel moisture, and pigments within them protect the wood from ultraviolet radiation. Any fresh applications soak in as well, rather than building up a coat on the surface.

A good door finish depends not only on how it's applied, but where it will be displayed.

■ DOOR PAINTING ART ■

Joe Bruneau of Brevard, North Carolina, is an artist who's been working in mixed media for years. But it wasn't until Jessica Claydon of Touchstone Gallery—where he'd been showing some baskets—commissioned him to paint her door that he considered that an avenue of expression.

In August of 1989, in the midst of a sidewalk art festival, Bruneau simply plucked the door from its hinges and set it on a couple of sawhorses. Over the three-day event, he sanded and primed the wood and applied oil-based paint over that, mounting the door back in place every evening when he left. Both sides of the door are painted, and sealed with two topcoats of clear varnish.

Another door, commissioned by Mary and Stephen Vieira on the basis of the first one, was painted in acrylic over antique oak. For those who might want to try their own hand at it, Joe suggests they start with a sturdy, solid, clean door and use a broad-based palette of colors. He usually works with a theme, the gallery door greeting "Homage to our paying customers" and the house door sticking with the yellow brick road motif to match the masonry.

The designs wear well but are protected only by the varnish, so they're not forever. When it's time to repaint, Joe takes it in stride: "It's only sealer for the wood—I can take it off or do it completely different the second time around."

The door is removed from its hinges and cleaned (or lightly sanded), then primed. Hardware can be covered or removed, and glass can be masked if needed.

The foundation color is set down in acrylic paint over the entire door, followed by major design elements, shown in accent colors at the door's upper corners and glass border.

Smaller elements are added at this point over the foundation and within the individual designs.

The smallest elements are applied last, as shown in the outlining and detail work in the border and images. Clear varnish protects the entire door, and the edges should be sealed in some way.

CHAPTER 8

HARDWARE

JUST AS THE NAME IMPLIES, door hardware indicates the metal parts—the hinges that allow it to open and the lockset that keeps it closed. Knobs, escutcheon plates, and other accessories also fall into the hardware category.

Hardware can be bought off the shelf at—where else?—hardware stores or home centers where you can special-order unique designs and finishes that may not be available in regular stock. Truly distinctive hardware, such as the samples shown on page 46, can also be custom-made here and by a blacksmith, using hand-forging and other traditional methods.

HINGES

By and large, doors pivot on butt hinges with removable pins. Sometimes, the pins may be attached to decorative ball tips which can be threaded in rather than held with the more common press fit. Other styles based on the butt design include T-hinges and strap hinges, used for a rustic look or when more support on the door is required; double-action hinges that allow the door to swing both ways; and specialty hinges such as the swing-clear offset type that carry the entire door out of its frame.

Mortise hinges—the kind used on most every door—have both leaves mortised or recessed, one into the door and one

into the jamb. Surface hinges are merely installed onto the surface of the door and jamb without any mortising. Half-mortise and half-surface hinges have only one leaf mortised—the former to the door, and the latter to the jamb.

The number of hinges required on a door is based on the size of the door, its weight, and whether it's an interior or an entry unit. Doors 5 feet or less in height and lightweight interior doors can use two hinges. Doors over 5 feet high require one hinge for each 2-1/2 feet of height. Standard 80" entry doors and heavy interior doors usually need three hinges. See the accompanying chart to determine the actual size of the hinges needed.

The hand of a hinge is determined from the outside of the door to which it is applied. If it opens from you to the right, it takes a right-hand hinge; to the left, a left-hand hinge. However, if it opens toward you to the right, it uses a left-hand hinge; and if toward you to the left, a right-hand hinge.

Hinges are laid out once the door has been fitted. When installing hinges, first position the leaves on the edge of the door. Traditionally, the upper hinge is placed 7" from the top, and the lower hinge 11" from the bottom. Otherwise, center both hinges 7" to 10" from each end. If a third hinge is

There's no dearth of door hardware for the custom door builder.

■ DOOR HINGE SIZES ■

Door Thickness	Door Width	Hinge Size
1" to 1-3/8"	To 32"	3-1/2"
1" to 1-3/8"	32" to 37"	4"
1-3/8" to 1-7/8"	To 32"	4-1/2"
1-3/8" to 1-7/8"	32" to 37"	5"
Over 1-7/8"	37" to 43"	5" Extra heavy

Hand-cast door hinges can be a work of art in themselves.

This elaborate brass door latch exemplifies the detail possible in door hardware.

used, it's centered between the two.

The hinge leaves should project enough to allow the knuckles to clear the trim or casing. Scribe around the hinge on the edge of the door with a sharp pencil. Then, with a sharp chisel, cut in along the marked line only to the depth of the hinge leaf. Remove the waste material by paring it away from the ends inward. You can use a router to remove the material, but you must still cut the outline first and might want to use a router fence to guide you past the long edge.

LOCKSETS

There are basically three different kinds of locksets used on doors, and a number of variations. Most common is the cylindrical lock, also called a tubular lock in a less complicated form. These are bored locks, meaning that holes must be drilled through the face and end of the stile to install them. The cylinder contains the tumbler mechanism into which the key fits.

Two types of latches are used with cylindrical locks. The first is a simple spring latch that enters the hole in the strike plate mortised into the jamb of the door, but is not positively engaged. It can be pushed back from the outside with a small, flat tool, and, because of this, it's not a good choice for an entry door. The second is the dead-locking latch. It has an additional piece alongside the bolt called a guard bolt that remains retracted even when the bolt itself has slipped into the strike plate. This guard locks the bolt in place so it can't be moved except by turning the handle.

Cylindrical locks can also be keyless passage latches, which have no locking mechanism and are commonly used on closet doors, or they can be privacy latches, which also have no keys, but can be locked from one side.

Locksets are centered 36" from the floor, or 38" in commercial buildings.

New locksets are supplied with a template that allows you to accurately mark all the holes that need to be drilled. If that's not the case, just measure up from the floor the required distance, then strike a horizontal line across the edge at that point. Then use a square to carry the line across to the face of the door and mark. Measure the backset—the distance from the face plate of the latch to the center of the knob—and mark that as well. A 2-3/8" backset is for a standard latch, but one with a 2-3/4" backset is available too, to place the knob a bit farther from the door jamb.

Normally, the large face hole is bored first, and a hand brace with an expandable bit can be used for this. Don't go all the way through in one pass, but rather complete the cutting from the opposite side, using the hole made by the tip of the bit as the new starting point.

The smaller hole can be drilled with a regular auger bit or spade bit. Drill all the way through horizontally until the point breaks out into the larger hole.

Then place the latch unit into the smaller hole and mark around the four sides of its face plate with a pencil. Cut along the pencil lines with a sharp chisel, and remove the waste to the depth of the face plate by paring it off with the end of the chisel. Once the latch unit is screwed into the edge of the door, each half of the cylinder and knob mechanism can be installed, then fastened together through the door itself.

The strike plate is positioned and installed after the door is hung. Mark the centerline of the latch bolt against the door jamb, and mark the edge of the bolt with the door pressed against its stop. Then position the plate over the marks and scribe its outline with a pencil. Mortise the jamb to the depth of the strike plate, then use an auger to drill the recess for the bolt. The bore

■ CUSTOM HARDWARE ■

Steve Kayne has been a blacksmith for a good part of his life, as it should be for someone who comes from four generations of smiths and apprenticed at his grandfather's knee from the tender age of eight. Kayne & Son Custom-Formed Hardware began as a business in Smithtown, New York, and ended up in Candler, North Carolina, some 40 years later, with sojourns at shows, festivals, and even a 30-day demonstration at Rockefeller Center in between.

Door hardware is only one part of Kayne's work, for he renders originals and reproductions of fireplace tools, Colonial accessories, and utensils, and does restoration work as well. Burning eight tons of coal a year in his forge, Steve uses hot-rolled mild steel and old traditional welding methods to work his craft on a European ornamental-ironwork anvil with a 1,000-year-old heritage that's a difference in night and day from the English shoeing design we see in old TV westerns.

For doormakers, shops such as Kayne's provide a wealth of quality and creativity simply not available from a store shelf. Iron and brass castings, intricate iron basketwork, and working reproductions of period hinges and handles—or even custom-designed pieces—could turn a door into a masterpiece.

Steve Kayne, busy working on a hinge at his coal-fired forge.

A door handle with detailed basketwork.

The Kayne showroom door displays some of the staff's handiwork.

can be cleaned up and squared, if needed, with a small chisel. Don't cut away too much material or you'll risk undermining the strike plate screws.

Many exterior and entry doors are equipped with a dead bolt in addition to the regular cylindrical lock. These can be placed anywhere from 6" to 11" above the existing knob and are installed in the same manner as the regular lock. They can be keyed on just the outside, with a small knob inside, or keyed on both sides. Once the bolt is thrown, it can be retracted only using a key or the knob.

A mortised lockset is a sturdy and costly unit used on thick and heavy entrance doors for top-notch security.

The handle is separate from the cylinder, but both are contained in the same unit. Because it fits into the lock stile in a deep mortise several inches long and close to 1" in width, it requires a good deal of skill to install correctly. Mortised units are almost always designed for a handed fit, depending upon which way the door opens.

To install a mortised lock, measure and mark the centerline of the handle at the desired height. Measure the backset and mark the centerline of the cylinder. Then measure and mark the door edge for the top and bottom of the lock case (not the face plate), and strike a vertical centerline in pencil.

With that done, use an auger or spade bit to drill the knob and cylinder holes through the face of the door, taking care to drill from both sides to avoid tearing out the wood. Then use a drill just larger than the width of the lock case to bore a series of vertical holes into the edge the depth of the case. This cavity can be cleaned out with tedious chisel work, then the face plate can be outlined and mortised in place before installing the handle and cylinder lock.

The third kind of lockset is a surface lock, mounted directly on the face of the door. These are easy to install and are often used for period restoration or to impart a rustic look. Usually the only hole that penetrates the stile is an opening for the knob shaft and a small keyhole. The lock box and the catch box are mounted to the door and the interior jamb with screws or lag bolts. Because of the tentative nature of the installation, surface locks are the least secure of all the locksets and may be useful only on interior doors or outbuildings.

Steve Kayne's pine-board foyer door is secured by his hand-forged strap hinges on one side and horizontal battens on the other.

CHAPTER 9

SELECTING YOUR STOCK

WOOD HAS A TIMELESS QUALITY that makes it appealing to woodworkers and homeowners alike. It's firm and straight, yet still can be worked into gentle curves and shapes. It can be finished to show off an attractive grain, or covered to hide an unattractive one. And it's warm and alive, flourishing in varied species.

But wood does have its mysteries. Those who have felt a bit out of their element in a lumber yard know too well that there's more to a board than its size. And the different wood species can be difficult to evaluate, let alone identify, without some seasoned guidance.

Certain kinds of wood are more suited to doormaking than others. The criteria that follow will help you to make the right selection, whether you're purchasing lumber from a retail yard, a home improvement center, or a custom wood supplier.

THE SIGNIFICANCE OF SPECIES

Wood has characteristics that make it a natural material for building. But what gives pine a different set of properties than oak?

All wood is made up of cellulose (the framework of the cells), lignin (the cement between the cells), organic extractives (which give the wood its color, density, odor, and resistance to rot), and trace minerals.

Variations in these elements make the difference between hard and soft woods, stiff and flexible woods, and woods that are light or dark. The makeup of each species is relatively constant, so a wood's species has come to serve as a criterion in selecting wood for one purpose or another.

Trees are classified in two categories, hardwoods and softwoods. But these

The author sights down a length of stock in preparation for planing it.

names can be misleading. A softwood such as Douglas fir or southern pine is actually harder than basswood, which is categorized as a hardwood.

Commercially available softwoods include pines, spruces, firs, and redwood. Hardwoods harvested for market include oak, birch, maple, cherry, and walnut.

For basic construction, commercial softwoods are good because they're readily available, reasonably priced, and easy to work with. Most lumberyards or home improvement centers should have a dimensional lumber on hand for framing and finishing the less complicated doors you'd want to build.

Commercial hardwoods—used for flooring, cabinetry, and furniture manufacture—are more expensive and not as easy to come by, though some

retail and millwork outlets supply them for home and hobby use. You'll have more access to hardwoods if you live in an area where timber is harvested, because independent suppliers such as sawmills and small manufacturers are plentiful in these areas. Sawmills are also a good source for softwoods and noncommercial lumber that is part of the trade in a certain locale. Cypress, larch, sweetgum, and sycamore are examples of some species that might be available in a local market.

Hardwood is a bit more difficult to work with than softwood because it's harder and more dense. That attribute is compensated for by the fact that hardwoods offer a cleaner cut, are usually stronger, and have better appearance quality than softwoods in general.

WEATHER RESISTANCE

Some species of wood are better at resisting decay than others. But all wood eventually succumbs to a fungi-induced rot brought about by the effects of moisture and exposure to the elements. Proper finishing and siting will allow a door to last many lifetimes, so decisions about which species to choose shouldn't be heavily based on its resistance to decay.

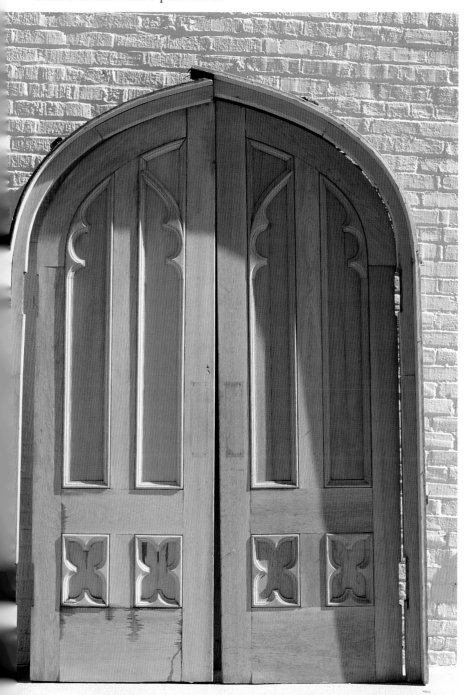

Even the panels and moldings of this American Gothic chapel door were cut in oak, and attest to its suitability as choice door stock.

Naturally decay-resistant woods are can be costly and often difficult to come by. Wood from a long-lasting species such as black locust makes good fence posts but isn't prized for door stock because it's exceptionally hard and difficult to work with. The exotics—mahogany, teak, and walnut—are resistant but quite expensive.

Redwood or cypress might be good middle ground since they are generally available and not too high-priced. In yard lumber, Douglas fir is ideal because of its moderate cost, strength, workability, and resistance.

Treated woods are not a good choice—because of their appearance and quality—unless the door faces regular weather exposure on an outbuilding or cellar entrance. When shopping for treated wood, you should know that there are normally two degrees of treatment—a light-density retention level (.25 lbs. per cubic ft.) for above-ground use, and a heavier-density level (.40 lbs. per cubic ft.) for below-ground applications. The higher-rated grade is slightly more expensive but will last longer for outdoor use. You should be aware that the toxicity of pressure-treated lumber remains in question, and the cautious woodworker would wear a dust mask when cutting it.

SIZING & DIMENSIONS

All lumber is sized and priced by its rough mill-sawn dimensions. But when the rough stock is planed, or surfaced, for the market, the overall size can be reduced by 25% or more. The original sawn dimension is called its nominal size—after planing, the piece is sold by its actual dimension. If you've ever wondered, this is why what's called a 2 X 4 really measures only 1-1/2" by 3-1/2".

A piece of lumber less than 1" thick and between 2" and 6" wide is called a strip. Stock less than 2" thick and up to 16" wide is a board. Dimension lumber measures from 2" to 4-1/2" thick and up to 16" wide, and timbers have a 5" dimension on any surface.

Standard lengths range from 6' to 16', in 2-foot increments.

Hardwoods are sized differently. Boards come in random widths up to 6", though larger widths can be custom cut. Standard lengths run from 4' to 16'. Thickness is generally measured in 1/4" graduations, from 1" to 4", and is expressed as a fraction—for example, a 5/4" board measures 1-1/4" before it's planed.

Hardwood and softwood are sold at the mill as rough when unplaned, or surfaced when planed on one or more sides. A board labeled S2S indicates that it's been surfaced on two sides.

Wood is sold in volume by the board foot, a long-established standard by which each unit is equivalent to a rough board measuring 1" thick by 12" wide by 12" long, or 144 cubic inches of wood altogether. The rules are that any stock less than an inch thick is counted as a full inch, and anything over 1" is figured to the next larger 1/4".

In practice, 4 board feet could be an 8-foot-long 1 X 6 or a 16-foot piece measuring 1-1/2" X 2". To calculate board feet, multiply thickness by width in inches, then multiply by length in feet and divide by 12.

Plywood—made of thin veneers glued so that the grain of adjacent layers runs perpendicular to one another—comes in a standard 4' X 8' panel. There is a 3/16"-thick panel, then sizes run from 1/4" to 3/4" in 1/8" increments.

GRADED LUMBER

Lumber is wood cut from trees, which is sawed and sold by standard dimension. When a log is harvested, the lumber varies in quality. To assure that buyers get a product that's suited to their needs, the lumber is graded into standardized categories.

The grade is based on the size of the wood and the number and significance of defects (knots, pitch pockets, decay) that affect the strength, utility, or durability of the finished product. Hardwood and softwood are each graded further by use, which takes species, appearance, and structural integrity into account.

■ DIMENSION LUMBER CHART ■

DIMENSION LUMBER STANDARDS AND BOARD FOOTAGE

nominal size (inches)	actual size (inches)	board foot @ length in feet				
		8	10	12	14	16
1 X 2	3/4 X 1-1/2	1-1/3	1-2/3	2	2-1/3	2-2/3
1 X 3	3/4 X 2-1/2	2	2-1/2	3	3-1/2	4
1 X 4	3/4 X 3-1/2	2-2/3	3-1/3	4	4-2/3	5-1/3
1 X 6	3/4 X 5-1/2	4	5	6	7	8
1 X 8	3/4 X 7-1/4	5-1/3	6-2/3	8	9-1/3	10-2/3
1 X 10	3/4 X 9-1/4	6-2/3	8-1/3	10	11-2/3	13-1/3
1 X 12	3/4 X 11-1/4	8	10	12	14	14
2 X 4	1-1/2 X 3-1/2	5-1/3	6-2/3	8	9-1/3	10-2/3
2 X 6	1-1/2 X 5-1/2	8	10	12	14	16
2 X 8	1-1/2 X 7-1/4	10-2/3	13-1/3	16	18-2/3	21-1/3
2 X 10	1-1/2 X 9-1/4	13-1/3	16-2/3	20	23-1/3	26-2/3
2 X 12	1-1/2 X 11-1/4	16	20	24	28	32
4 X 4	3-1/2 X 3-1/2	10-2/3	13-1/3	16	18-2/3	21-1/3
4 X 6	3-1/2 X 5-1/2	16	20	24	28	32
6 X 6	5-1/2 X 5-1/2	24	30	36	42	48
8 X 8	7-1/4 X 7-1/4	42-2/3	53-1/3	64	74-2/3	85-1/3

■ PLANNING FOR CHANGES ■

There's no getting around it—lumber shrinks and changes its shape as it dries. The shrinking process occurs as moisture evaporates from the wood's swollen cell walls; this begins when the moisture content drops below 28% or 30%. Any water lost prior to that comes from the hollow cell cavities and doesn't affect the lumber's dimensions.

The changing process develops as a result of where within the log the boards were cut from (see the illustration). Since wood cells are in the form of growth rings, with their length vertical like the trunk, shrinkage varies considerably in thickness, width, and length. The latter is almost negligible—less than 2/10%—but shrinkage across and around the growth rings is considerable. Cross-grain (radial) shrinkage averages 4%-5% from green to oven-dry in oak, Douglas fir, and other door-worthy species. In the direction of the rings (tangentially), shrinkage is about twice that.

Unequal shrinkage in all directions is what causes the bowing, twisting, cupping, and crooking that ruins an otherwise good piece of lumber.

Even after the wood is dried and installed, the relative humidity within an environment can make big changes. Wood picks up moisture in high humidity and gives it off when humidity drops. Inside a home, where temperatures through the seasons are fairly constant, but humidity levels may vary by 30% or 40%, this puts a lot of pressure on wide door panels and other parts particularly affected by change. The moisture content of this wood can easily double between dry winter and humid summer, changing the dimension of the panel by a full 1/4" or more.

The unhappy result is exposed paint lines where panel meets stile, or swelling so great that the joints between rails and stiles are broken. Allowing door panels to float freely with ample clearance in the frame grooves, and using low-permeability finishes on the wood help considerably with this fact of life.

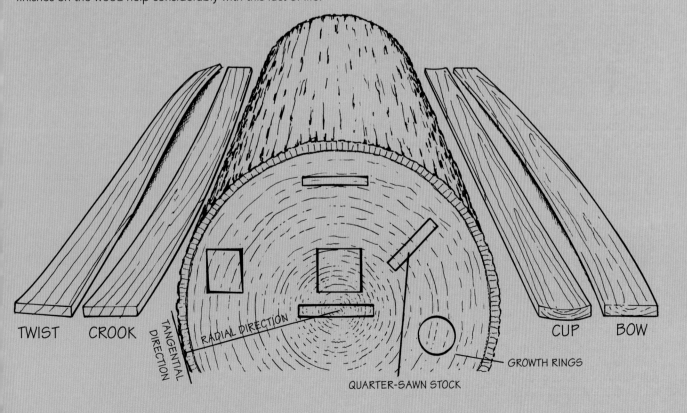

TWIST   CROOK   TANGENTIAL DIRECTION   RADIAL DIRECTION   CUP   BOW

GROWTH RINGS

QUARTER-SAWN STOCK

Softwood grades have been established for construction. Common lumber is yard stock used for general building purposes and includes boards, planks, and lath. The boards fall into five different grades depending upon species. No. 1 has tight knots and minor blemishes and is used for finish work; No. 2 has larger knots and noticeable blemishes and is suitable for flooring and paneling; No. 3 contains knotholes and visible flaws, fine for sheathing and fencing. Nos. 4 and 5 are low-quality boards. Some manufacturing associations use names rather than numbers to assign grades: "Colonial," "Sterling," and "Standard" correspond roughly to the top three number grades.

Appearance lumber isn't graded for stress, but has visual appeal for finish work. Select grades are described by letters and numbers: B & Btr (1 and 2 Clear) is a higher quality product than C Select, which contains limited defects. D Select grade has minor surface imperfections. Certain species are named by the labels "Supreme," "Choice," and "Quality."

Hardwood lumber is graded into categories, mainly for manufacturing. There'd be little reason to have mill-cut wood graded for a door project, but just so you know, "Firsts and seconds" (FAS) is a combination of the two best grades—the boards must be at least 6" wide and 8' long. "Selects" are FAS-quality boards at least 4" wide and 6' in length.

Plywood panels can be constructed of softwood (Douglas fir, western hemlock, and pine) or hardwood (birch, oak, cherry, and walnut).

Plywood grades are established by the quality of the face and back veneers. The inspection stamps on the back of each panel show the grade of both sides, the wood species group number (lower numbers indicate stiffer panels), application for interior or exterior use, and the mill and testing marks.

Softwood panels are graded by letter: N—suitable for a natural finish and free of open defects; A—smooth and paintable, limited to 18 neatly made repairs; B—solid surfaced, with circular repair plugs and tight knots; C—knotholes up to 1" and tight knots to 1-1/2", with limited splits allowed.

Hardwood panels use number grades: 1-premium—book-matched grain with only minor defects; 1—good, but unmatched grain and minor defects; 2—sound, suitable for painting, with appearance defects and smooth patches.

What's the Best Choice?

In lumberyard wood, the better grades will be free of major defects, but it's always a good idea to visually inspect the lumber you want before you buy it. Some yards try to discourage "hand-picking," but you should expect to get what you pay for.

Things to be critical of in a piece of wood are knotholes, checks, wane (flat or rounded edges), and warpage—either a bend or a twist in the wood. If appearance is a prime concern, as in hardwoods, the existence of pith, stain, or insect holes can affect your choice.

Workability of the wood is important, but with sharp-bladed tools, problems can be minimized. A dense softwood such as southern pine or Douglas fir will cut and work well; hardwoods, especially oak, are tough on tool edges but have the same good qualities. The species to avoid are those that tear easily, are prone to split and warp, and give a ragged cut.

With rough-sawn wood, the amount of water it contains is a factor of its finished quality. Fresh-cut wood can have a moisture content of 50% or more of the wood's oven-dry weight. As drying forces the water out of the wood, it begins to shrink. If it's not dried evenly or consistently, the wood can warp and bow.

Both kiln-dried and air-dried lumber are affected not only in the drying process, but also by the wood's location within the original log (see "Planning for Changes"). By the time the lumber gets down to a workable 19% or lower moisture content, one in ten boards may be damaged. Buying mill lumber that's already been dried will cost you more, but you will at least be able to see exactly what you're getting.

Conserving a Renewable Resource

Even though you might think that the ecological aspects of woodworking may not play a big role when you're puttering around in your shop, there's no denying that real threats exist to old-growth forests in South America, Indonesia, and even in the Pacific Northwest and Appalachian regions of the United States.

As a woodworker, you may not be able to change the world in a weekend, but there are a few things you can do to slow down the wanton destruction of old forest resources and conserve what we have left both on the stump and in the shop.

First, use recycled wood and components. Not only are manufactured and salvaged pieces fair game (see page 57), but consider such sources as oak pallets, old billets, and even deadfall from local trees.

Second, make an effort to seek—and then buy—certified wood products where applicable. These are labeled woods that have been taken from overseas and domestic sources where sustainable forest management has been practiced.

Finally, work your wood wisely. Use thinner saw blades where you can, and use a bandsaw to make resawn stock from solid pieces if possible. Cut your wood close to the line in preparation for planing and finish work. And think about time-proven techniques such as veneering over particleboard and fiberboard. You can even build your embellishments and bolections from smaller molding components rather than cutting then from a single hunk of wood.

CHAPTER 10

PREPARING YOUR WOOD

GOOD WOODWORKING HABITS are built on accurate stock preparation. Regardless of how fine your tape measure and square may be, wood that doesn't have square edges and straight, parallel surfaces to start with is certain to result in doors with the same characteristics.

A good door begins with the right preparation.

If you're not using a millwork shop for preparation, read this chapter carefully. Stock that is dressed—cut, planed, and edge-jointed—improperly produces ill-fitting joints and mismatches progressively down each step of assembly. But the machining of stock involves more than just running wood through a few pieces of equipment.

First, before you begin cutting, you need to have a clear idea of your project. This not only means how it will fit together—and a cut list with a rough plan sketch can help with that immensely—but also how the pieces will blend when the door is complete. Grain direction and colors that complement or match should be a key goal in this planning stage. If at all possible, gather your materials at the same time and from the same source, figuring in a little extra if possible. Nothing can be more frustrating than the lack of a single kindred component from an otherwise perfectly planned project.

Second, you need to recognize the hazards involved in cutting raw wood. One is that your board may not be flat, which puts unequal pressure on the thickness planer. The other is that there are internal stresses in the wood due to growth patterns or the drying process. These can pinch a rotary blade, causing dangerous kickback.

The normal routine is to first cut the boards to length, leaving a few inches extra for trimming. Then the stock should be jointed and planed, ripped to width, and finally cut to finished length for use in the door.

Sometimes, the order of things is changed if there's a long piece of stock with an imperfection such as a cup or bow. In that case, it may need to be crosscut into shorter pieces—or ripped

into individual strips—before it can be planed safely. It's not all that unusual for a lower-grade large board to be pieced-out like this in order to render a number of high-quality smaller boards.

Once stock has been cut to rough length, it can be surfaced in the direction of the grain. Wood cut against the grain invites tearout and ultimately produces a rough surface, even after sanding.

The best way to determine grain direction is to first look at the curvature of the growth rings at the end of the board to establish which was the inside face, then—with that face up—the V-pattern that's visible points in the correct direction. On the opposite, or outside, face of the board, the correct direction is just the reverse.

Four feet, more or less, is the ideal length for jointing and planing, but exceptions must be made for major door components, which are longer than that. Avoid machining short pieces (less than 16")—these should be done as part of longer stock.

~ Face-jointing is the process of using the jointer to remove high spots on the face of a board. When surfacing cupped or bowed stock, the concave side should rest on the table so the edges or ends touch first. These will be the first to be removed, until the board is uniformly flat. If the distortion is severe, remove the high parts first with a hand plane, then make light, gradual passes over the jointer blade to avoid taking too big a bite at one time.

~ The thickness planer "reads" the board's one flat side and makes the opposite side parallel and uniform. Once the first side is planed, the board should be turned over and planed again, since the planer makes a smoother cut than a jointer. To maintain consistency, you should plane all your stock of the same thickness at one time before changing the machine's setting to make the next series of cuts. Shaving the wood's outside layers may alter its moisture content enough to cause minor distortions in the board. If that happens, the stock should be set aside for a week or so until it reacclimates to its environment, then resurfaced.

~ Edge-squaring is done on the jointer. If the board is crooked, the bad edge must be removed first. A hand plane can take off the high ends, but in severe cases, the edge of the board must be cut. There are several ways to do this, but one of the safest is to snap a chalk line between the ends as a guide, then use a jigsaw to cut along the line. Square the jointer by checking its fence against the cutter head with a reliable square, then pass the stock through the machine with its edge positively against the table, and its face positively against the fence.

~ Ripping, or cutting to width, takes place on the table saw. Always put the board's jointed edge against the fence to give the most accurate cut. On pieces that require accurate surfacing on all four sides, add 1/16" or so to the final edge to allow for jointing later.

~ Final cutting for length is done on the table saw, or with a radial arm or miter saw. The initial cut squares one end, and the second cut establishes the finished length. On longer members, such as door stiles, it may be impractical to rely on the short miter gauge to make an accurate final cut.

Prominent bolection molding and twin arched etched-glass panels speak well for this salvaged entry door.

CHAPTER 11

MILLWORK

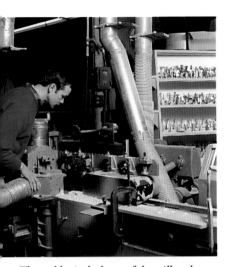

The molder is the heart of the millwork shop. Small shops can provide custom ripping, planing, and jointing services, too.

Any wood that has been machined by planers, shapers, cutters or mills of various types is referred to as millwork. Moldings, sashes, trim, appliques, dentils, columns, brackets, and stair parts are all examples of milled pieces that—in the heydey of master joinery—were cut by hand, on site, with specialized tools.

These days, all of these parts can be ordered through a catalog in a variety of common softwood and hardwood species. And the ease with which a machine could make those intricate cuts did not escape our woodworking forebears, who took the opportunity to harness motors for this kind of work almost immediately. Much of the Victorian-era fret work, and the architectural accouterments following that period, were mass-produced and mail-ordered for later installation.

For the astute doormaker, small independent woodworking shops can be a gold mine when it comes to millwork. As interest in restoration and sensitive rehabilitation continues to flourish, it's not just banks, churches, and municipal buildings that benefit from the craftsmens' skills. These local mills have become a prime source, as well, for the intricate millwork that typifies residential reproduction and architectural woodwork.

Detailed moldings, fluted trim, dentil work, corner blocks, and a variety of other machined wooden pieces can make a fairly ordinary door stand out as something special. As you peruse the photos of the many doors shown throughout the book, you'll be able to glean some ideas for your own use of milled stock.

DOUBLE CLASSIC PROFILE

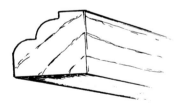

COPE-AND-STICK PROFILE

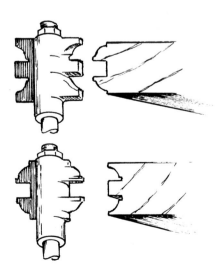

BEADED PANEL CUTTER PROFILE

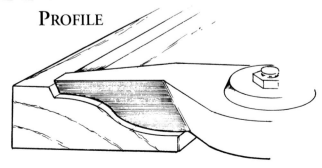

Forest Millwork employee Marty Noble checks the blueprint for the front door to his arts and crafts home.

■ FOREST MILLWORK, INC. ■

There are probably hundreds of small millwork shops around the country, yet how many people know exactly what goes on inside them? Two people who do are Bill Hamer and Alan Tenan who've owned and operated Forest Millwork, Inc. of Asheville, North Carolina, for the past five years.

What keeps them busy? Mostly architectural woodwork for churches, financial institutions, and government buildings. They service the general contractor whose job it is to get the best work at a reasonable price for his client.

Much of their work involves duplication of doors, windows, molding, and trim for the larger jobs, along with casework and other cabinet-style manufacturing. Mostly domestic woods are bought in lots by the job to avoid the problems of mismatching and running short of stock.

A quick look through an open door wouldn't tell you as much, but machinist Robert Davis fills in the details of what it takes to please a customer: He operates the molder that can cut a profile of any shape desired into a strip of wood, and in fact part of his job is to design and grind the custom knives for his machine (see photo). That tool, plus the bandsaw, jointer-planer, pin router, drum and machine sanders, and several saws allow the production shop to hum along and keep more than a few employees busy.

But there's still time for the smaller jobs, because custom cutting isn't always in the realm of the general woodworker.

There are literally dozens of knife profiles available for the machines' cutter heads.

CHAPTER 12
ARCHITECTURAL SALVAGE

WITHOUT A QUESTION, old doors are the most commonly sought after architectural items, and this book wouldn't be complete without mentioning them. For, far from being in competition with the idea of building new, a sound door from years past can lend a degree of authenticity to a home full of modern equivalents.

When you recycle a door, you not only make use of something that might otherwise go to waste, but you're getting the best of the bargain: old joinery techniques, unique detail work, and the patina of age can't be recreated perfectly at any price. And, especially with interior doors, there's not a whole lot that can go wrong with them that can't be set right. At best, a joint may have to be reglued or the finish restored. Obvious distress such as splits, warpage, and drill holes can be evaluated and tackled if you have the inclination.

As nice as an old door may be by itself, it's even nicer when accompanied by its original hardware. Even if you can't locate the hinges, knobs, and escutcheons that may have come with that particular door, you can make period replacements of those parts work just as well, if not better, to suit your needs.

When shopping for period doors, look to salvage specialists, warehouse dealers, and even antique shops. These aren't the kinds of things you'd normally find at flea markets and garage sales.

Try, if at all possible, to acquire the jambs, trim, and corner blocks, and any accessories that went with the door, as these are important architectural elements that will probably have to be recreated later if they're not taken now.

Also, salvaged items need not be limited to door stock. A good salvage dealer or savvy demolition contractor will save timbers, flooring, and framing members from the wrecker's ball for reclamation. In most cases, the wood from old houses, commercial buildings, warehouses, and the like are full-dimension lumber in desirable species such as oak, maple, hickory, heart pine and Douglas fir. This wood, once de-nailed and planed, can provide some of the most spectacular door stock available, and sometimes at extremely reasonable cost.

Doors galore…and many other architectural items greet renovators at a well-stocked salvage shop.

■ PRESERVATION HALL ■

The heart of downtown Asheville, North Carolina, harbors one of the best examples of true architectural salvage around, a business aptly named Preservation Hall. Owned and run by Ivo Ballentine and Robin Cape, with son and daughter Django and Lucy, it's been the gathering place for several years for rescued doors, mantels, staircases, and related architectural antiquities.

Ivo, a born recycler who's been professionally involved in salvage for nearly a decade, sticks mainly to the local area to retrieve his stock because of its rich architectural history. Even with demolition imminent, Ivo works for historical preservation with city authorities to save valuable architectural elements whenever possible.

Since customers can come from quite a distance—some even with shopping lists—the Ballentines combine the occasional long-distance delivery with a buying trip to investigate the local artifact scene in other cities. Currently, the family is restoring one of the oldest buildings in Weaverville, North Carolina, and plan to open a new store and gathering place at that location.

Ivo Ballentine rescues for reuse much of his community's architectural heritage.

Antique door knobs and locksets to satisfy every desire.

Escutcheons, face plates, and other door hardware waiting to make a close match or a perfect fit.

THE PROJECTS

CHAPTER 13

LOOSE-TENON PANEL DOOR

> **Overall Dimensions:** 33" X 80"
> **Stock:** Douglas Fir 1-1/2" X 5-1/2"
> **Stock Finished Size:** 1-3/8" X 5"
> **Style:** Two-panel frame and panel

SUGGESTED TOOLS

Table saw

Dado blade

3/8" drill

1/2" spade bit

Router

1/2" fluted bit

7/16" classical ogee bit

1/2" chisel

Block plane

Straightedge

Tape measure

Try square

Pipe clamps

Hammer

Coping saw

Backsaw

Miter box

Palm sander

CUT LIST

2	Stiles	1-3/8" X 5" X 80"
2	Rails	1-3/8" X 5" X 23"
1	Kick rail	1-3/8" X 10" X 23"
1	Panel	1/2" X 24" X 24-1/2"
1	Panel	1/2" X 24" X 37-1/2"
6	Tenons	1/2" X 3" X 5-3/4"
8	Rail molding	7/16" X 5/8" X 23"
4	Stile molding	7/16" X 5/8" X 23-1/2
4	Stile molding	7/16" X 5/8" X 36-1/2"

HARDWARE AND SUPPLIES

16-gauge X 1-1/4" finish brads

Waterproof aliphatic resin glue

3" swing-clear hinges

Lever and latch set

A DOOR'S STYLE is often dictated by its surroundings, and this is especially important in older historic homes where renovations are made to harmonize with the existing architecture. Unless carefully planned, a new door will stand out as a modern afterthought, regardless of how well it functions.

I made this door for a grand old home that was built in the 1880s and just recently converted to offices for a doctor's practice. Federal law requires a minimum 32" clearance for wheelchair access, but a 32" door would not have been acceptable because the 1/2" door stops reduce the actual access opening to 31" in width. Conversely, a 34" or larger standard size was not an option because the load-bearing framing at that entry could not be modified economically. The custom-sized 33" door, hung on swing-clear hinges (in which the leaves are offset to carry the entire door out of the frame), answered the need for both handicap access and a style that would match the rest of the house.

Previous page: Twin faux-screen French-style doors with astragal. These are an adaptation of the project door described beginning on page 80.

This panel door was made to accommodate an extra-width opening while maintaining the building's character.

The frame and panel door is the most ubiquitous of door styles. It consists of a frame, or perimeter, of solid wood in a rail-and-stile configuration with thinner wood panels or plywood set into a rabbet or groove within the framework. Solid wood, if used across the entire face of the door, would be affected by the contraction and expansion that comes with cold weather and direct sunlight. Since the panels "float" inside the frame, this natural movement can occur without affecting the perimeter of the door and causing it to bind or gap. A paneled door is also considerably lighter than a solid one, saving the need for heavy hinges and reducing the risk of sagging.

The advent of the 1/2" router and the selection of specialty bits made for it have put the frame and panel door within the ability and cost range of the average woodworker. The joints at the rails and stiles still need to be held together, and using a simple loose tenon—as I did in this door—is one of the easiest ways of doing that. Other reliable methods include doweling, mortise-and-tenon, and modern biscuit joinery. The panels can be held in place with trim or bolection molding and rabbets, or grooves.

You'll have to take the dimensions of the door opening to come up with an accurate materials list. Then, on graph paper, draw out the door's configuration, indicating all parts and sizing them to the proper dimensions. On a standard 1/4"-grid sheet of 8-1/2" X 11" graph paper, using a scale of 1/4" = 2" will allow you to fit the door plan onto a single sheet. Transfer the sizes of the 2 stiles and 3 rails to a cut list, then roughly estimate the size of the panels from your drawing. The kick rail on this door is a full 10" wide, so 2 X 12 dimension lumber is required for that. The panels can be made from 1 X 10s and planed down to 1/2", unless you plan on raised panels, which call for a piece of stock between 3/4" and 1-1/2" thick.

Door construction is not all that complicated. The rails and stiles provide strength and support; the panels fill the openings between.

THE PARTS OF A DOOR

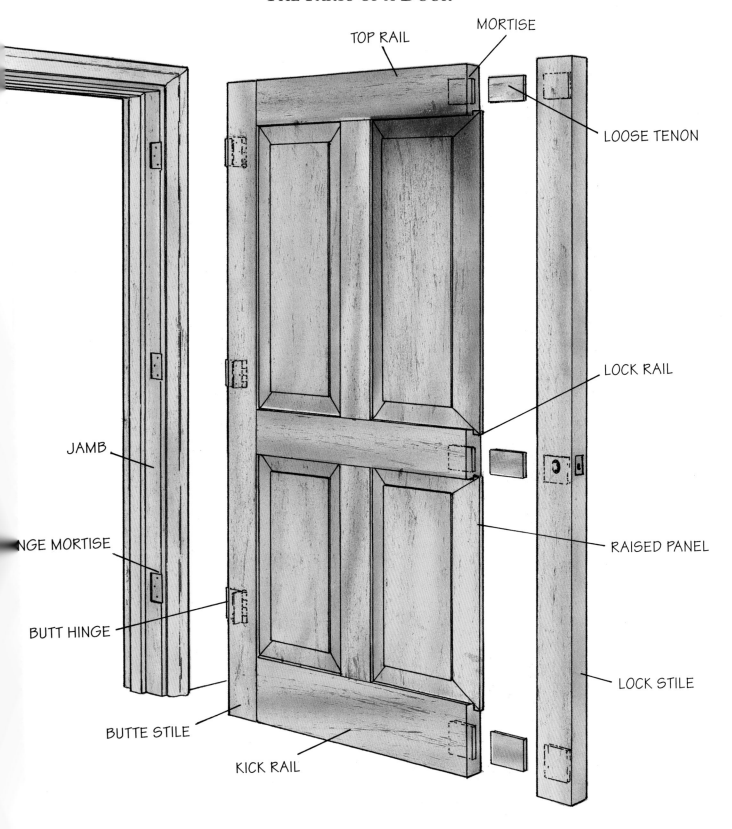

MORTISE

TOP RAIL

LOOSE TENON

JAMB

LOCK RAIL

NGE MORTISE

RAISED PANEL

BUTT HINGE

BUTTE STILE

LOCK STILE

KICK RAIL

Loose-Tenon Panel Door

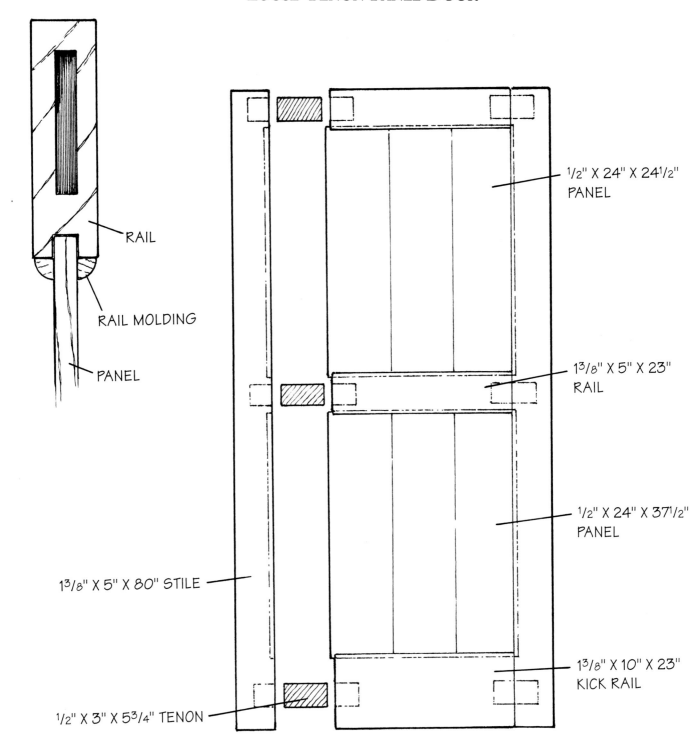

RAIL

RAIL MOLDING

PANEL

$1/2$" X 24" X $24^1/2$" PANEL

$1^3/8$" X 5" X 23" RAIL

$1/2$" X 24" X $37^1/2$" PANEL

$1^3/8$" X 5" X 80" STILE

$1^3/8$" X 10" X 23" KICK RAIL

$1/2$" X 3" X $5^3/4$" TENON

FIGURE 1

FIGURE 2

CONSTRUCTION PROCEDURE

1. Crosscut all the frame parts to a bit over finished length, planning around knots and avoiding checks at the ends. Use a jointer to surface one edge and one face of the framing members, or have a local millwork shop prepare it for you. Plane the stock down to 1-3/8". With the surfaced edge facing the table saw fence, rip each rail and stile 1/8" greater than the finished width, then plane to size.

2. Plane the panel sections (or have them planed) to 1/2", then lay out the panels, alternating the grain patterns to keep the finished pieces from cupping. Cut the edges on a table saw (or use a jointer if you have access to one), then edge-glue the pieces to make the two panel sections, using pipe clamps alternated at the top and bottom surfaces.

3. Cut the stiles and rails to exact length, making sure the crosscuts are square. Lay them on the workbench as the door is to be configured. Mark the location of the rails against the stiles. Turn the stiles so the inside edge is facing upward and use a square (Fig. 1) to transfer the marks across that edge. Then mark a centerline on the stiles.

4. To mark the locations for the tenons, measure 1" in from the top and bottom of the 5" rails and 3-1/2" in from the top and bottom of the 10" kick rail. Repeat the procedure using the marks on the stiles for reference. Use a 1/2" spade bit (Fig. 2) to drill holes 3" deep at both ends of each marked mortise to define its opening.

5. Use a long 1/2" fluted (or straight-cut) bit in the router to remove material between the holes to complete each mortise. Clamp the stiles and 5" rails together with the tops flush to provide a flat working surface. If you have a router fence, use it to center the cut exactly. Set the router depth to remove up to 1/2" material in each pass and complete all the stile mortises.

6. To run the rail mortises, clamp the rail ends in a vise along with a section of 2 X 6 to make a flat working surface (Fig. 3). Complete cutting the ends of each rail (Fig. 4), being aware that end grain requires extra care in cutting.

FIGURE 3

FIGURE 4

7. Make the tenons from stock planed down to 1/2". Rip the planed stock to 3" in width, then cut the individual tenons to 5-3/4" in length, or 1/4" shorter than the total depth of each mortise. Sand, or round the tenon edges over with a roundover bit, then dry-fit the components (Fig. 5) to check for binding or looseness. Sand the meeting edges (Fig. 6) of the frame members at each joint so the corners are rounded slightly for a better appearance (Fig. 7).

8. Disassemble the door components and turn the stiles inside edge up. Measure 1/4" and 1/2" beyond the inner rail edge marks at each joint and make two marks. Use a 1/2" Forstner bit to drill 1/2"-deep holes at the 1/4" points. Then use a try square to carry the 1/2" marks to one side of the stiles.

Next, set the dado blade to a 1/2" thickness and a 5/8" height, and adjust the saw fence so the blade will be centered in the edge of the 1-3/8" stile. Mark, on the table saw's throat plate, the point at which the blade protrudes above the surface (Fig. 8). Then cut 1/2" X 5/8"-deep slots in each piece between the 1/2" drilled holes using a plunge-cutting technique, directing the stock into the top of the blade so the throat plate and side marks align before feeding it forward. Cut 1/2" X 5/8" straight-through dadoes into the inner edges of the rails that accept panels.

9. Cut the panels to length and rip the side edges if necessary to allow 1/8" to 1/4" clearance all around within the frame dadoes. Radius the corners of each panel with a coping saw slightly to eliminate any interference at the joints. At this point, you can sand and apply finish to the perimeter of the panels to make sure a finish line isn't exposed with weather changes.

10. Begin gluing on one stile by applying aliphatic resin to the stile mortises (Fig. 9) and the three rail mortises. Apply glue to the tenons (Fig. 10), then insert the tenons (Fig. 11) and the rail members (Fig. 12). Insert the panels and finish gluing the opposite ends of the rail and the remaining stile. Clamp the completed frame at each rail with a pipe or bar clamp, and check the assembly for square by measuring from corner to corner. Wipe away any excess glue with a damp rag.

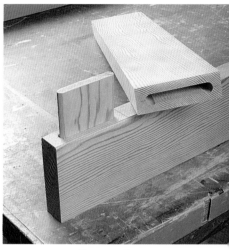

FIGURE 5

FIGURE 6

FIGURE 7

FIGURE 8

FIGURE 9

FIGURE 12

FIGURE 10

FIGURE 11

■ Panel and Molding Details ■

Rabbet and Flat Panel

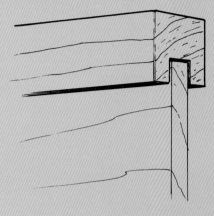

Rabbet and Flat Panel with Bolection

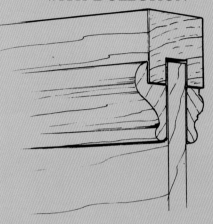

Rabbet and Flat Raised Panel with Molding

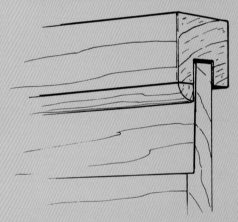

Rabbet and Curved Raised Panel

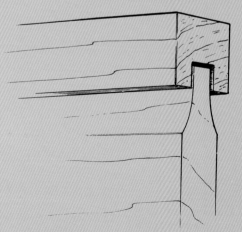

Stop Molding and Glass with Bead

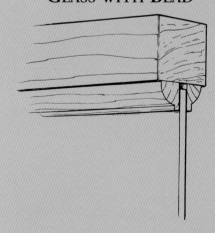

FIGURE 13

to give the frame a smoother look. Fit the door into its opening to check for clearances.

14. Apply the sealer and paint or finish (Fig. 14) as desired (refer to Chapter 7 for specifics).

15. Hang the door using the techniques described in Chapter 17.

■ OPTIONS

There are a number of panel choices for this type of door, and you shouldn't be limited by the availability of standard stock in a lumberyard. The design of a raised panel requires a board at least 3/4" thick, and preferably closer to 1-1/2" so the panel will be on the same plane as the door frame itself. The panels can be cut on a table saw (see the bifold door on page 91) or shaped with a profiled panel bit using a 1/2"-collet router. For flat panels, a good cabinet-grade plywood is fine for a paint finish, or you can use a two-sided veneered sheet for stained finishes. Medium-density fiberboard (MDF) is an excellent choice for painting and it can be machined quite nicely, as well.

The slots that house the panels were cut with a dado blade in this door, but as in most woodworking projects, there's more than one way to accomplish the same task. A 1/4" X 5/8" slot-cutter bit in a router can make the groove in one or more passes with the door frame temporarily clamped in position. Working from the centerline, 1/4" of material is first cut from above the line, then the entire door can be flipped over and the process repeated to remove wood from the other side of the line. This will create a 1/2" centered slot 5/8" deep. Internally, the corners will remain radiused, so they'll have to be chiseled clean or the panel corners cut to fit.

FIGURE 14

11. After overnight drying, unclamp the door (Fig. 13) and check it for square and level on a flat surface. Sand the wood with a medium-grit paper and remove any dried glue from the joints.

12. You can make your own profiled molding from 1/2" X 5/8" stock with a 7/16" classical or other ogee-style router bit, or you can purchase milled stock. Cut the vertical stile moldings on one side to length with 45-degree miters, then predrill nail holes every 6" or so and use 16-gauge X 1-1/4" finish brads to fasten the moldings to the reveals on the side of each stile. Measure the rail moldings for individual fit, then miters those cuts at the appropriate length. Fasten the rail moldings using the same method. Turn the door over and follow the same procedure to install the moldings on the opposite face.

13. Finish sanding the entire door, starting with a 120-grit paper and continuing down to an extra-fine 220-grit, particularly if you're applying a natural finish. You can round over the edges and corners with the sander beforehand

CHAPTER 14
SPLINE-JOINTED BATTEN DOOR

> **Overall Dimensions:** 33-1/4" X 74"
> **Stock:** White Oak 8/4" X 8"
> **Stock Finished Size:** 1-3/4" X 6-11/16"
> **Style:** Five-board with Z-brace batten and arched top

SUGGESTED TOOLS

Table saw

3/8" drill

1/8" bit

7/32" bit

3/16" bit

5/32" bit

1/4" bit

Countersink

Phillips bit

Jigsaw

Backsaw

Router

1/4" X 5/8" slot cutter bit

45-degree chamfer bit

3/4" chisel

Straightedge

Level

Tape measure

Try square

Block plane

C-clamps

Pipe clamps

Hammer

Palm sander

CUT LIST

2	Stiles	1-3/8" X 5" X 80"
5	Boards	1-3/4" X 6-11/16" X 74"
2	Battens	1-1/2" X 9" X 31-3/4"
1	Diagonal	7/8" X 4" X 41-3/4"
2	Side jambs	1-1/8" X 5-3/8" X 77"
1	Head jamb	1-3/4" X 4" X 34-1/2"
1	Head jamb	2" X 4" X 34-1/2"
1	Head jamb	1-5/8" X 4" X 34-1/2"
1	Cap board	1" X 5-3/8" X 35-1/2"
2	Door stop	5/8" X 2" X 72-3/8"
1	Threshold	1-1/2" X 11" X 33-1/4"
4	Splines	1/2" X 1-1/16" X 72"

HARDWARE AND SUPPLIES

1/4" X 2-1/4" Distressed lag bolts

1/4" X 3" Distressed lag bolts

No. 10 X 3" Deck screws

6-penny finish nails

4-1/2" Butt hinges

Mortise lockset

Waterproof aliphatic resin glue

*A century-old log cabin was the perfect
setting for this heavy batten door and
its matching screen.*

EVEN THOUGH THIS STYLE is
technically a batten door, I've been
referring to it as "the cabin door" since
I agreed to take on the design and
building project more than a year ago.
So many beautiful rustic homes and
buildings in rural environments are
blemished with manufactured prehung
doors that do not even begin to complement the structures to which
they're attached.

This style door is perfect for rustic
cabins and log homes in country or
suburban settings. With some simplifi-
cation, the design can be used for sheds
and outbuildings that deserve more
than a sheet of plywood on hinges.

The log cabin I designed this door
for was built sometime in the 19th
century, nestled in an open mountain
draw alongside a flowing creek. The
owner wanted a solid, bear-proof door
and had already been disappointed
once in his dealings with a contractor
who came to prepare a bid and then
ignored the difficult job.

I knew from previous historic renovations that this project would be a challenge. Since the rough opening
contained masonry chinked around
what passed for head and side jambs,
and a sloping threshold besides, I took
measurements in every direction I
could think of, and reluctantly brought
out the level to confirm my plumb-
and-squareness fears.

After perusing a few of my sketches,
the owner chose an arched-top design
that agreed well with the cabin but was
also the most difficult to configure.
Because he wanted a heavy door,
I had to forgo the recycled fir I often
use, and instead search for a decent
straight-grained 8/4 white oak.
Although the full 2" material was
expensive, I found an ample supply at
a local hardwood dealer and picked
through the stack choosing candidates
with the straightest grain.

Even after all my paper planning,

SPLINE JOINTED BATTEN DOOR

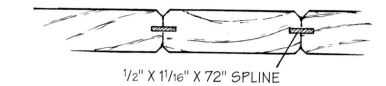

$1/2$" X $1^{1}/_{16}$" X 72" SPLINE

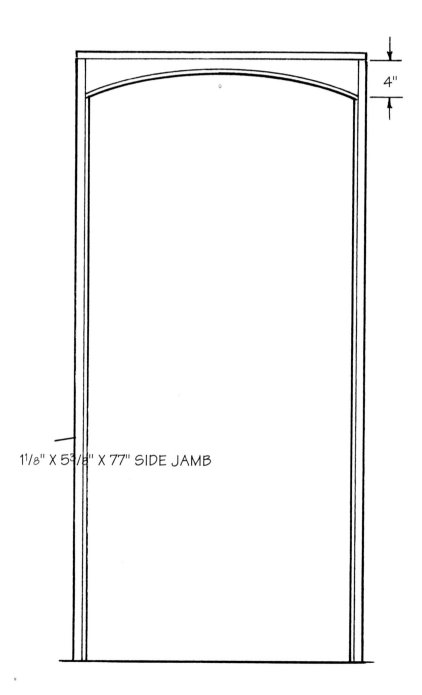

4"

$1^{1}/_{8}$" X $5^{3}/_{8}$" X 77" SIDE JAMB

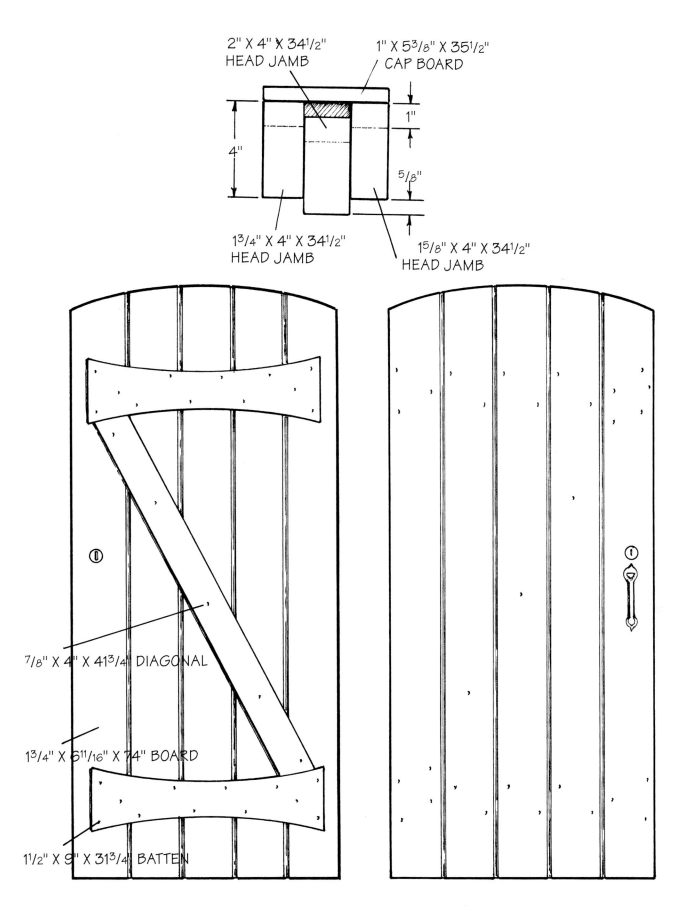

2" X 4" X 34¹/₂"
HEAD JAMB

1" X 5³/₈" X 35¹/₂"
CAP BOARD

1"

4"

5/8"

1³/4" X 4" X 34¹/₂"
HEAD JAMB

1⁵/₈" X 4" X 34¹/₂"
HEAD JAMB

7/8" X 4" X 41³/4" DIAGONAL

1³/4" X 6¹¹/₁₆" X 74" BOARD

1¹/₂" X 9" X 31³/4" BATTEN

I came up short one board in the middle of the project and had to return to the dealer, only to discover he'd sold the rest of the load to someone 500 miles away. I lost a full day calling on other suppliers, and finally found one willing to sell a single board, and that at a healthy premium. I should, of course, have purchased the whole stack for a flat figure and been done with it.

Since this door was a good half-foot shorter than normal because of the nature of the building, I was able to use 14-foot lengths of wood to get two verticals from one board. This kind of careful planning can save quite of bit of material in one project, though care should be taken when buying full lengths of rough-sawn lumber (see page 51).

The batten, or Z-braced door, as it's sometimes called, can be a good first-door project if it's built with a traditional square top. Actually, the basic technique used in this door can lead naturally to a frame-and-panel door if you need a design that's a little more modern and adaptable.

The frame-and-panel door is nothing more than a framework made up of stiles and rails rabbeted at the inner edge to accept tongue-and-groove panels inset in this rabbet. A whole variety of looks can be achieved by assembling the panels in different configurations, as shown on page 119.

Traditional batten doors were simple to build and were used on barns and sheds where leakage at the joints wasn't a concern. Long nails were used to hold the battens or ledges to the vertical members, then the points were bent over, or "clinched" (see page 79) to the surface.

This modern batten door answers the call for an old-time rustic look and the need for a weather- and draft-proof access. It's assembled using splines or strips of wood fit into grooves cut along the inside edges of each vertical board. Only one side of each spline is glued in

■ COMMON BATTEN DOOR PATTERNS ■

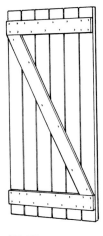

Z-BRACED

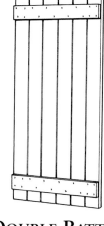

DOUBLE BATTEN

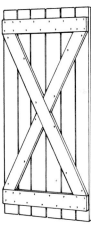

X-BRACED

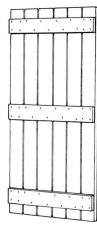

TRIPLE BATTEN

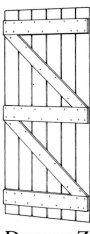

DOUBLE Z

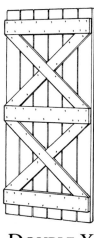

DOUBLE X

order to allow the necessary movement in such a massive field, as the door's surface is called.

Commercial tongue-and-groove stock can also be used, as there are a wide variety of widths and thicknesses available, made with beaded, veed, or plain-butted joints. And the field can be double layered and aligned vertically, diagonally, or horizontally to create a thicker door with a double-faced feature.

The rough opening must be considered before you begin any design work. If the existing jamb is in decent shape, you may be able to pull dimensions off the old door. First check to see that it fits the opening with no gaps larger than 1/4" to 3/8". Use a level to gauge the jamb for plumb in both directions—front and side—then for level at the head and threshold. If it is out more than 1/2" top to bottom, you'll need to adjust it or possibly replace it depending upon its condition.

If you plan to rebuild the jamb, you'll need to allow 3/4" to 1" overall from framing member to framing member, and slightly less at the head. This will help you in shimming and leveling, covered in more detail in the door installation chapter on page 99.

The arched top is an unusual feature and will be explained in the construction proceedures that follow. It's simpler to make the jamb first and build the door to that established radius than the other way around. A slight arch usually works best as it's easier to cut. If you want to build a similar-style door with a square top, just exclude the trammel compass and marking steps and make the head cut square.

*A screen door was made to match
the design of the entry door.*

CONSTRUCTION PROCEDURES

1. Lay out the vertical boards and figure how wide each needs to be to span the face without having one that needs to be ripped more than a third the width of the others. Ideally, you should plan on taking material from each board's edge to get the overall width you need. Place your battens and figure on setting them back from the door's edges 3/4" or so in order for the door to close properly. Their position from top to bottom is a matter of appearance, based on how wide and tall the door is. A distance of 6" to 8" from the bottom and slightly more from the top usually give the door the proper proportion. The diagonal batten should be narrower and slightly thinner than the horizontals, and a few inches longer than needed to allow for trimming.

2. Prepare the stock by jointing and thicknessing to the desired dimensions, or have a millwork shop do it. Then set each board out, good side facing one direction, to plan the finished look of the door with regard to grain pattern. Number each piece in pencil to correspond to its position on the door. Set the unit aside to prepare the jamb.

3. The jamb components should be of the same material as the door to keep the look consistent, and thick enough to support its weight—6/4 oak planed down to 1-1/8" suits this project. The width, especially with a log home, may be greater than usual because of log diameter, and this also allows for a screen door even if one isn't planned right away.

Make a trammel compass by first locating a long flat stick about 1/2" thick, an inch or so wide, and up to 10' in length. Drill a pencil-diameter hole in one end of it and insert a pencil in the opening. If the trammel is longer than your workbench, you'll have to set up a stand or sawhorse at the same level as the bench and center the horse at one

end. Then spread a sheet of heavy paper on the bench to match the width of the door and head jamb. By moving the trammel up or down, you'll be able to establish a pivot point on the bench (or sawhorse) that gives the desired arch on the paper plus the 9/16" ears on the ends. Once the point's been established, mark it with a small hole and fasten the trammel loosely with a screw or pin.

The head jamb consists of three pieces joined side to side. Each piece needs to be wide enough to equal the span between the low part of the arch and a point one inch above the top of the arch. Square and center each head jamb piece in position on the workbench and mark the arches with the trammel. Cut the arches close to the line with a jigsaw, then sand the cuts square.

4. Glue and clamp the 1-3/4" jamb board to the 2" jamb board so that the arched edge of the thicker piece extends 5/8" below the edge of the other member to create a door stop. Measure 5/8" down from the lower corners of the 1-3/4" jamb board, mark lines parallel to the upper edge, and cut the corner points from that piece. Drill two rows of staggered 3/16" holes 6" apart through just the 2" jamb board. Countersink the openings. Then use an extra-length 1/8" bit to drill pilot holes into the 1-3/4" piece. Fasten with No. 10 X 3" screws.

5. Glue and clamp the 1-5/8" jamb board to the screw-head face of the 2" piece, allowing a 5/8" rebate as on the opposite side. The upper edges of the outside members should be even; there will be a 5/8"-deep channel down the center of the assembly because the 2" jamb board is recessed. No screws are used on the 1-5/8" face, but a cap board can be installed and fastened to the top edges with countersunk screws if the rough opening allows clearance.

FIGURE 1

FIGURE 2

6. Cut 9/16" X 4" dadoes into the corner of each side jamb to let in the completed head jamb. This can be done with a dado blade or repeated passes on the table saw followed by some chisel work. The door stop extends below the 4" line; mark it and, again using a chisel, mortise out a relief on both jambs for this piece.

7. Set the head jamb into the side jambs and cut a scrap strip to temporarily hold the lower ends of the jamb the correct distance apart. Tack the strip to the bottom ends, then drill and fasten the jambs to the head using two No. 10 X 3" screws per side.

8. Cut the two side stops and install them to the jambs in line with the head stop. Predrill the mounting holes and fasten the stops with 6-penny finish nails or recessed No. 6 X 1-1/4" screws. If nailing, wax the points and be especially careful not to split the wood.

FIGURE 3

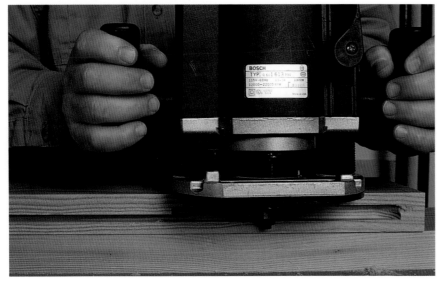

FIGURE 4

9. Use a piece of posterboard to make a template of the cuts at the jamb's threshold end. Carefully measure the width of the jamb, and the size and position of the stop, cut out the template, and transfer the marks to both ends of the threshold board by reversing the paper. Set the table saw to cut a 15-degree bevel, then adjust the saw fence to start the high point of the threshold just under the edge of the door to assure positive rainwater runoff. Allow a 1-1/2" flat surface for under the door, then flip the board over and cut the interior bevel. Use a backsaw or jigsaw to cut out the notches for the stops.

10. Clamp the door boards together, leaving the surface unobstructed and making sure the top and bottom edges of the door are aligned. Using the same trammel setup as before (Fig. 1), recreate the identical arch in pencil across the top of the door (Fig. 2), making sure to transfer the curve so as to match the finished jamb's height. Cut the door top squarely with a jigsaw (Fig. 3), staying just above the line. Sand the cut edge square.

11. Separate the door and use a square to mark lines across the joining faces of each board 1" from the top and bottom ends. Rip the 1/2" plywood splines to 1-1/16" in width, then cut to the individual length needed for each joint.

12. Measure the exact thickness of the plywood splines (they should be a fraction smaller than the nominal 1/2"), then set up the slot-cutting bit in the router to make the initial cut for each joint. (A dado blade in a table saw will accomplish the same thing.) First draw a line between the end marks straight down the center of each edge, then use that as a reference to cut below and above. (Set up on a test piece first to establish that the spline is neither too loose or so tight that it needs to be driven in.) Cut the grooves into each adjoining edge between the marks (Fig.

4), then cut or round-over the corners of each spline to fit against the uncut radius left at the groove ends by the router bit. Dry-fit the splines (Fig. 5) and plane them slightly if needed (Fig. 6) at the points where they're too tight.

13. Chamfer the interior corners of each adjoining board by 1/4" or so to break up the flat field. This should be done on the full length of both faces of the board, using a 45-degree chamfer bit in the router, or simply by hand with a block plane (Fig. 7).

14. If you plan to flare, or curve, the horizontal battens, establish the radius using the trammel. The reverse arch is a matter of preference, but the curve should be no tighter than the arch of the door itself. Extending the length of the trammel stick by a factor of 1/3 will produce the arch shown. Mark the curves on both edges of each batten, then cut with a jigsaw. Use a 45-degree chamfer bit in the router to put a 1/2" chamfer in the face edges of both battens.

15. Glue the splines to one side only of each joint member to allow some freedom for expansion and contraction caused by changes in weather. Align the door and clamp it together, from underneath if possible at the center and from the top at the ends. Make certain all the boards are square and aligned.

16. Use C-clamps and wood-scrap pads to position the two horizontal battens and the diagonal, which must run up from the bottom hinge to help support the weight of the door. Fasten the horizontals first, by turning the door over with its face (outside) up and carefully marking the location for each screw. A full-scale paper template of the battens can be used on that side to help gauge the position of the fasteners—two per board, three for the end boards.

Whether using lag bolts or flathead wood screws as fasteners, the clearance holes in the boards must be snug—but

FIGURE 5

FIGURE 6

FIGURE 7

not too tight—to prevent racking. Test-drill some holes in a piece of scrap to check beforehand. If flathead screws are used, they must be countersunk to the same depth by using a stop collar. With the clearance holes drilled, use a 2/3-smaller bit to drill the pilot holes into the battens. Drive in the fasteners, but be certain that they're not so long that they penetrate the batten faces on the other side.

17. Prepare the diagonal by fitting it in place and scribing a pencil mark to match the curves in the battens. Cut the ends to match with a jigsaw, then use a 45-degree chamfer bit to put a 1/2" chamfer in the face edges of the diagonal, leaving 2-1/2" uncut at the ends. Fasten the diagonal to the door in the same manner as the battens, keeping in mind that it's not as thick and requires shorter fasteners.

18. Remove the clamps and sand the entire door, starting with a medium 80-grit paper and working down to an extra-fine 220-grit sheet. Finish the wood as you like, referring to Chapter 7 for guidance if needed.

19. Hang the door in the jamb and install the hardware. Chapters 8 and 17 explain these procedures in detail. The 1-3/4" stock chosen for this door allows the use of a mortise lock, that fits completely within a cavity mortised in the lock board. Often, strap hinges were used on batten doors because they help hold the verticals together, but in this project, three 4-1/2" ball-tipped butt hinges were used.

■ **OPTIONS**

Clinched nails are a classic fastener for this type of door, as they were the primary method of applying battens before—and well after—reliable and affordable screw fasteners were developed. To use them, choose galvanized finish nails suited, by length, to the thickness of your stock. They should penetrate the door and protrude beyond the wood by 1/4" or so. Locate and predrill the nail holes, using a bit no more than half the diameter of your nails. Set the nail heads, then turn the door over and clinch, or bend, the nail points over into the wood using the nail set, following the grain pattern to seat the point properly. If need be, back the nail heads from beneath with a hardwood block while clinching to prevent the nails from backing out.

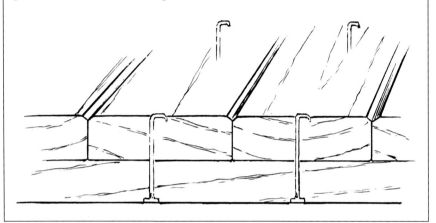

Chapter 15

Tenon-Jointed Screen Door

> **Overall Dimensions:** 41-1/8" X 90-1/2"
> **Stock:** Clear Fir 1-1/2" X 5-1/2"
> **Stock Finished Size:** 1-3/8" X 4-1/2"
> **Style:** Upper screen with center rail and lower panels

Suggested Tools

- Table saw
- Dado blade
- 3/8" drill
- 1/2" Forstner bit
- 3/16" bit
- 1/8" bit
- Phillips driver
- Router
- 1/4" X 1/2" slot cutter bit
- Jigsaw
- Circular saw
- 1/2" chisel
- Block plane
- Straightedge
- Level
- Tape measure
- Try square
- Pipe clamps
- Hammer
- Nailset
- Spline tool
- Utility knife
- Miter box
- Backsaw
- Palm sander

Cut List

2	Stiles	1-3/8" X 4-1/2" X 90-1/2"
1	Center stile	1-3/8" X 4" X 26-1/2"
2	Rails	1-3/8" X 4-1/2" X 33-1/8"
1	Kick rail	1-3/8" X 9-1/2" X 33-1/8"
2	Panels	1/2" X 15-1/2" X 27-1/4"

Hardware and Supplies

- No. 10 X 6" drywall screws
- 16-gauge X 1-1/4" finish brads
- 1/8" screen spline
- Waterproof aliphatic resin glue
- Half-surface spring hinges
- Latch set

Simple tools and a series of procedures were used to make this paneled screen door with removable storm glazing.

I LIKE TO THINK OF THIS as another door with special appeal to the beginner because it can be made mainly with a table saw, using standard clear select (B- or C-grade) 2 X 6 stock and A-C exterior plywood. The dimensions used in the instructions are for a standard 1-3/8"-thick door, but, since the recommended stock is actually 1-1/2" X 5-1/2" in size, the resulting door will be slightly thicker and sturdier than the screen doors you're probably used to. The difference can easily be compensated for in installation, but if you want a standard-thickness door, the stock should be planed beforehand.

This particular screen door was made to fit an oversize opening used in a cottage built around 1911. The portal's odd width and unusually tall 7-1/2-foot height dictated a custom-built door, a circumstance that has brought me a good deal of contract business. Thankfully, home centers and mass-marketers don't custom-fit entryways!

Having said the only major tool needed is a table saw, that assumes that you have access to straight, flat boards—true quarter-sawn lumber (see page 51) if possible. Should the stile pieces be crooked, you'll need to have them run through a jointer to remove the curve; edge-surfacing such as this can usually be performed by a local millwork or woodworking shop.

As an alternative, much the same thing can be accomplished using a long flush-cutting bearing bit on a router and a straight plywood strip as a guide. The strip is clamped to the board, allowing the router-bit bearing to follow the plywood edge, forcing the bit to remove the irregular stock.

A cupped board will likewise respond to a few passes through a thickness planer. This kind of dimensioning, again, can be contracted with an outside shop at reasonable cost if you don't have the equipment on hand to do it.

If it weren't for insects, dogs, and children, there'd be no need for screen doors. But as long as they're necessary, they should be planned to minimize their effect on both the entry door behind, and—in the larger picture—on the house as a whole. You should aim, for example, on arranging the rails on the screen door to match those on the main door if it has elements worth maintaining.

Often, practical matters dictate design. Lock sets can determine the width of the stiles, and the setback—the distance from the center of the knob to the edge of the door—can vary between manufacturers within a range of 1-3/4" to 2-3/4". Maintaining at least a 4" stile width is just good practice because it allows some leeway when drilling the bolt bore, which can easily penetrate the stile's screen edge if you don't use caution.

Prior to laying out the components, it's a good idea to take measurements at several locations within the doorway. Start vertically on both sides and in the middle of the opening, then measure horizontally at four or five locations from top to bottom. Record these on a small sketch of the opening, noting the locations.

The final measurments should be taken from corner to corner, both ways, to check for square. With any luck, these last two dimensions won't be dramatically different—if they're off by more than 1/4", you'll have to increase the length of the door by that amount and plane it to fit later to account for the variation.

When replacing a screen door, you'll notice that there's usually a rebate, or rabbet, in the jamb to allow the door to set within the frame. Measure the dimension of this rebate to gauge how thick to make your screen door. It's acceptable to make the door slightly larger than this dimension, but best to avoid having the unit project beyond the door trim, or it will be constantly exposed to rain.

If your jamb doesn't have a rebate, you can simply install door stop stock to frame the inner face of the jamb. To be safe, measure the distance between your entry door and the proposed screen location, being sure to allow room for the knobs of both doors to latch shut without touching before nailing in the stop. If clearance is a problem, you can offset the screen door knob up or down a tad, or consider fitting hardware with a slightly different profile.

Once you're satisfied that you've done a thorough job of planning, you can get on with the work. If this is your first attempt at fabricating a door, you'll find that laying out the project in full scale will help immensely. Refer to page 88 for a detailed explanation of this process—but meanwhile, simply think of it as using a pattern to check the placement and fit of the door components before you do any cutting.

The site-prepared boards on which these full-scale templates are made go by a variety of names, but setting-out rods, layout sticks, and story poles are three of the most common. It's true that it does take time to set up these layout aids, but doing so can save more time—and possibly a fair measure of lumber stock—later on.

That's because it's not difficult, in the course of making changes and striking measurements, to accumulate an overwhelming array of paper that does more to confuse than enlighten. A piece of 1/2" plywood measuring 12" X 96" is not only hard to lose, but offers a life-size reference that most people find easier to read than a scrap from a notebook.

This particular screen door uses an open tenon joint, so you'll need to include the 1/2" width of the tenon when calculating the overall width of the stile, since both components come from the same piece of wood (see Fig. 5). In practical terms, this means you'd have to start with 4-1/2"-wide stock to finish with a 4" stile. The 1/2" tenon is

TENON-JOINTED SCREEN DOOR

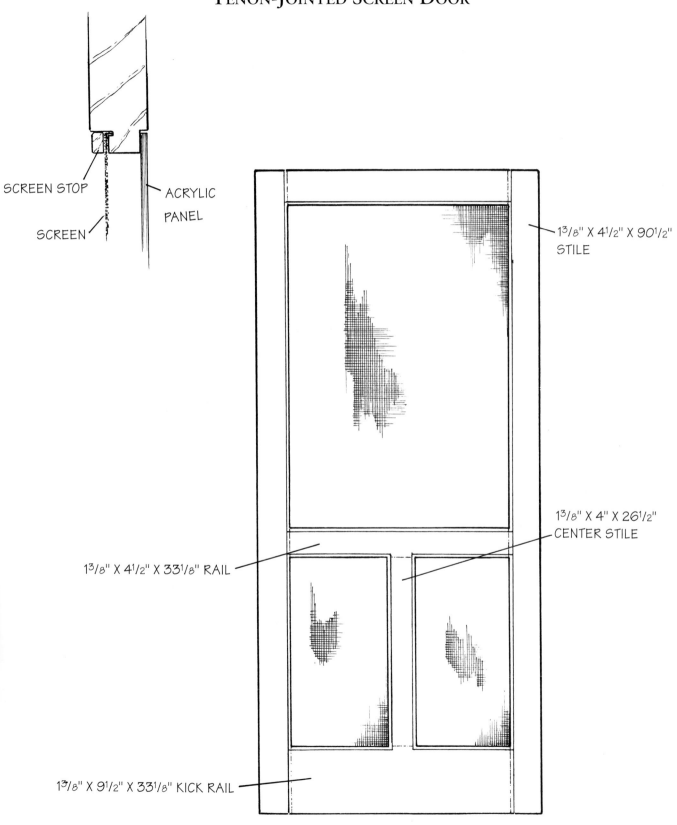

SCREEN STOP

SCREEN

ACRYLIC PANEL

$1^3/_8$" X $4^1/_2$" X $90^1/_2$" STILE

$1^3/_8$" X 4" X $26^1/_2$" CENTER STILE

$1^3/_8$" X $4^1/_2$" X $33^1/_8$" RAIL

$1^3/_8$" X $9^1/_2$" X $33^1/_8$" KICK RAIL

exposed (except at the joints) along the inside of each stile and functions both as part of the joint and as a receiver, or bed, for the screen spline and the removable storm window. The same pattern is duplicated, as well, on the two rails which hold the screening.

Before cutting the tenon profiles, it's important to match the diameter of the vinyl spline and the wire gauge of the screen you'll be using to your saw blade width. A 1/8" black spline and .011" dark aluminum screen work well in combination. The blade's kerf is positioned to accommodate the spline and screen, and they will not fit properly if the blade is too narrow or too wide.

To check this beforehand, run a test kerf 1/4" deep and several inches long about 1/2" from the edge of a piece of scrap wood the same dimension as the stiles you'll be working with—1-3/8" thick and 4-1/2" wide.

That done, set a piece of screen on the kerf and crease it slightly. Using the convex roller of the spline tool, make a few passes over the screening to start it into the kerf. Then place the spline over the screen and use the concave end of the tool to press the screen and the spline into the kerf bed. If it's difficult to do, or if the screen rips, you need a larger kerf or a smaller spline. Since vinyl is less expensive than saw blades, resizing the spline is a more practical approach unless you intend to buy a new blade anyway.

With your layout board and materials on hand (including some extra for test pieces) you can establish your own cut list, using the accompanying list as a guide. If one of the pieces needs to be wider than the rest (as in this door's kick rail), you'll have to edge-join two boards together or purchase a length of wider stock. It's a good idea to visually grade all the lumber before making any cuts, since careful planning around knots and imperfections can maximize wood usage. As you select the individual

pieces, label them by name (kick rail, butt stile, etc.) and by position (face, top, and so on) to avoid confusion. Light pencil markings will suffice here.

Look over your stock on a table that's large enough to hold the entire door. Pick out the stiles first, as these should be the longest, straightest boards. Plan for the best of the pair to be the lock stile, since this is the most prone to warp. Next, pick the good edge, or the one with the most vertical grain, to be the lock stile's outer edge. Finally, choose the board's good side for the face, or front of the door. By moving, rotating, and flipping boards, you can establish the look of your door, keeping grain patterns and color consistent if the wood will show through in a natural finish.

When making the initial crosscuts, leave each member an inch or so longer than the required dimension to make the parts more manageable. A radial arm saw or sliding compound miter saw is best for these first cuts unless the components are unusually wide, in which case a circular saw fitted with a fine-tooth blade and guided against a square or straightedge will do.

Also, if you need to install a door stop, now is the time to cut the material, before you begin the process of setting up the saw fence for the profiles which follow. Stops can be 1/2" to 3/4" thick and 1-1/2" wide. If there's a lot of variation in the jamb, the thicker stop will provide a better wind seal. One four-foot and two eight-foot pieces of stop stock is plenty for each door.

CONSTRUCTION PROCEDURE

1. Beginning with a two-foot test piece measuring 1-3/8" X 4- 1/2", set the table saw blade to a 9/16" height and the fence 4" from the inside of the blade. Run the test piece several inches into the blade, keeping it tight against the fence. Carefully withdraw the piece and check the kerf for depth and posi-

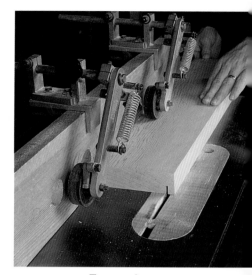

FIGURE 1

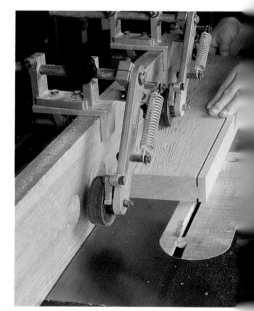

FIGURE 2

tion and reset the saw if needed. Once set, make this initial kerf cut on the face side of all the labeled 4-1/2" pieces that will receive screen (Fig. 1). Be careful not to lose contact with the fence on the longer pieces, especially at the ends.

2. Lower your blade to 3/16" and keep the fence where it is. You'll be flipping the pieces over to cut on the back side, making shoulders for the open mortise and starting a receiver for an acrylic storm panel. Run your test piece through the saw as before, check the cut, and make any adjustments. Then make the cuts on the back side of each 4-1/2" piece (Fig. 2) that will receive screen.

3. Set the fence to 3/16" from the outside of the blade, which is a change from the previous setups. Raise the blade to slightly less than 1/2" and run the test piece into the blade on edge, with the back side tight against the fence. Make sure the top of the blade makes full contact by running the piece several inches in. The object is to remove the small strip to create the receiver for the storm panel, and this must be done cleanly without leaving

any steps that might hamper the joining process. Complete the cuts on the edges of all 4-1/2" pieces that receive screen.

4. Set the fence 1" from the inside of the blade and leave the height where it is. This cut, again made on edge, will remove the screen stop pieces—which you'll save—and will leave part of the initial saw kerf made in Step 1 to receive the screen spline. It's possible to adjust the tenon size within plus-or-minus 1/16" by moving the fence slightly, but its thickness should be very close to 3/4". Pass the test piece through the blade with the back side against the fence. Check the thickness of the tenon and depth of the kerf left intact. Then cut the edges of all the 4- 1/2" pieces that receive screen (Figs. 3 and 4).

5. Cut the rails and stiles to their exact length (Fig. 5), as established in your initial layout. It's important that the rails are of equal length and perfectly square. To check the door width before cutting, you can lay the rails on top of the stile tenons to mark and measure. Do not measure from the ends of the tenons because they'll be

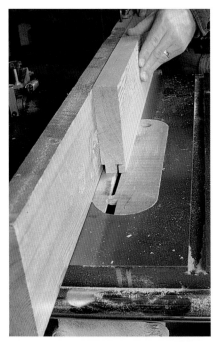

FIGURE 3

FIGURE 4

FIGURE 5

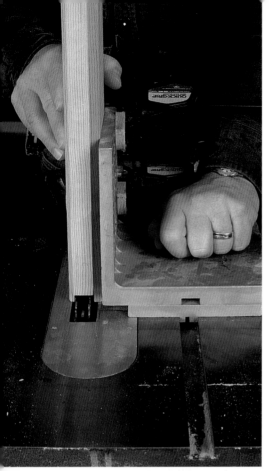

FIGURE 6

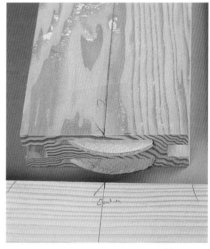

FIGURE 7

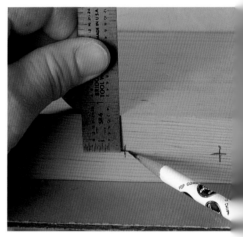

FIGURE 8

it for fit. Since the mortise is offset, it's important that all subsequent dado cuts be made with the work facing the same way. Complete the cuts on the ends of all rails, including the 9-1/2" kick rail.

7. Dry-fit the three rails and two stiles together on the table. If a joint is too tight, pare down the tenon slightly using a sharp chisel. Line all the pieces up and clamp the door together, then check for square by measuring the door both ways from corner to corner. Mark at the lower edge of the lock rail and the upper edge of the kick rail on both stiles. Disassemble the door.

8. Using a fine-tooth backsaw, cut through the tenons at the marks to a point just shy of the stile faces. Use a jigsaw to carefully remove the tenons between the cuts on each stile. A block plane and chisel can be used to smooth and square the cut faces. Reassemble, square, and clamp the door.

9. Install a 1/2"-deep, 1/4"-kerf slot-cutter bit into the router and set its depth to match the back side of the mortises already cut into the ends of the rails. Then carefully rout the inside edge of the door's entire lower frame. Raise the cutter bit to create a 1/2" mortise and repeat the procedure.

tucked inside the mortises when the door is assembled.

6. Now the rail mortises can be cut based on the actual size of the tenons. Measure in several locations along each stile to establish an average size. The critical points are at the ends, where the rails join. Install a dado blade on the table saw and set up the 1/2" depth (the bottom of the mortise should just meet the end of the tenon) and the 3/4" width (the fit should be snug but not tight). A mortising jig as shown in the photo (Fig. 6) will allow you to hold the work securely, or you can use a straight piece of 1 X 6 the length of the fence as a backer board to help prevent tearout of the wood at the ends of the mortise cuts.

Set the fence so that the back side of the work will be against it, at whatever distance from the blade is required to allow the mortise to match up with the tenons. Then run a test piece and check

FIGURE 9

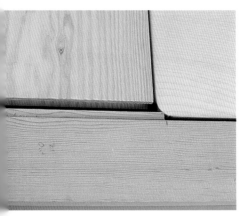

FIGURE 10

10. Cut the center stile to its exact length, being sure to account for the 1/2" tenons at each end. Position it over the mortised rails and mark the placement of the tenon shoulders. Using the same technique described in Steps 1 through 3, cut 1/2" X 1/2" full-width tenons into each end of the stile. These tenons are offset but do not require the kerf cut for the screen spline. (As an option, biscuit joinery can be used in place of the tenon if the centers of the lock and kick rail are left unmortised [Fig. 7].)

11. Locate the center of the mortised rails and clamp the stile at that point. Using the router and slot-cutter bit, rout a 1/2" mortise into both sides of the center stile using the procedure described in Step 9.

12. Mark a line along the outer edges of the stiles 11/16" from the face side (Fig. 8). Use this line to center two screws at each joint except for those at the lock rail, which get one each. The exact spacing and location can be adjusted somewhat so the screws will not interfere with the door hardware. Drill 1"-deep holes with a 1/2" Forstner bit at each screw point. Follow with 3/16" clearance holes drilled just beyond the end of the tenon (an extra-length 6" or 8" bit is needed for this

[Fig. 9.]). Then use a 1/8" extra-length bit to sink pilot holes in the rails to a depth of about 2".

13. Measure the two panel openings at the lower part of the door and include the depth of the mortises all around. Cut the panels on the table saw, then radius the corners slightly with a jigsaw (Fig. 10).

14. Disassemble the door and hand-sand the rails and stiles lightly. You can round-over the edges to add a nice touch to the joints if you wish. Clean off the dust and prepare to glue using a small flux brush. With a damp rag at hand, glue all the meeting surfaces on both the rails and stiles, install the panels, and assemble the components. Tap the joints with a block and hammer to align them as needed. Install the clamps and wipe excess glue from the joints, and check the door for square. Drive the No. 10 X 6" screws into place (Fig. 11), taking care not to overtighten and risk stripping the bores.

15. Use 1/2" tapered plugs glued in place to fill the screw holes. Leave the ends protruding slightly so they can be sanded flush later. You can also fill the small spline kerfs at the top and bottom edges of the door with waterproof wood filler.

16. After overnight drying, remove the clamps and sand the surfaces, starting with 80-grit paper and dropping down to a finer 120-grit sheet. If you plan on a natural finish, continue down to 220-grit, or until no scratches are visible.

17. The door can be fit at this point. Place it in the opening and shim the bottom to force it into the top of the jamb. The objective is to create a consistent reveal around the door of 1/8" to 3/16" at the top, 3/16" to 1/4" at the sides, and 1/4" to 1/2" on the bottom. Shim the sides as needed and note the areas that need trimming. Remove the door and clamp it on edge in the bench, then remove wood

FIGURE 11

■ USING A LAYOUT STICK ■

Accurate layout, or "setting out," is one of the surest ways to avoid mistakes in woodworking. It means making decisions beforehand about sizing, widths, joints, and design, and it forces the slothful to sharpen their planning skills.

Layouts are like a plan view—done full size, on 1/2" plywood boards (called rods or sticks) about 12" wide and 8 feet long or whatever length your intended door happens to be. One edge of the stick needs to be absolutely straight and smooth, and the board should be flat so as not to distort transferred lines. It's best if the surface is light-colored, and some even coat the wood with flat-white paint to show up pencil marks.

The best reason for using layout sticks is to avoid extra steps in figuring, since all dimensions are transferred to the door components directly. The other reasons are just as practical: the shape of members, the placement of joints, and the size of rebates, moldings, and details will be determined before you have a chance to make costly mistakes. You'll also be able to draw up a cutting list for your trouble.

A vertical (side) view is laid out on one side, and a horizontal (top) view rendered on the other side of the board. Though a marking gauge can be used to mark out the stick, it's much quicker and easier to use a steel rule, reading dimensions from the straight side of the board and letting the end of the rule serve as your pencil's marking guide.

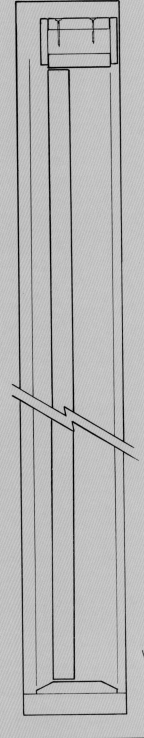

VERTICAL (SIDE) VIEW

HORIZONTAL (TOP) VIEW

FIGURE 13

FIGURE 14

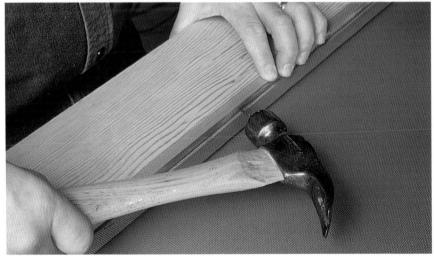

FIGURE 15

where needed with a plane. Reset and check the door. At the threshold, run a pencil flat along the inside to scribe a bottom line. Add the necessary top reveal (1/8" minimum) to that line, remove the door, and clamp a straight-edge to the kick rail, figuring in the distance between your circular saw blade and its shoe, and accounting for a 10- to 15-degree forward bevel if the threshold calls for it. Then lay the door flat on the table and carefully trim the bottom edge.

18. Re-sand any trimmed spots or surfaces that were marred in fitting. If you plan to paint the door, now is the time to seal or prime it, including the edges and especially the end grain. Paint the screen stops as well.

19. Lay out a section of screen and cut it 2" oversize on all sides. Start at the top, and using the spline tool's con-vex wheel, press lightly to crease the screen into the channel. Cut an appro-priate length of spline and using the concave wheel, run the spline into the groove using short repeated passes (Fig. 13). Repeat at the opposite end, pulling only slightly to tighten the screen. If the tension is even, secure the two sides in the same manner. Trim the screen (Fig. 14).

20. Miter one end of the screen stop so the smoothest edge faces outward. Set it in place and mark its opposite end for length and miter. Cut, and repeat this procedure for the remaining three stops. Nail them in place from the sides if possible (Fig. 15), using No. 16-gauge X 1-1/4" finish brads every 12" or so.

21. Cut the arcylic panel to fit the receiver on the inside of the door. Take measurements 1/8" smaller than the opening, and use an acrylic cutter for a clean edge. If you prefer tempered glass, take your dimensions to a local supplier and have it cut to order. Hold the panel in place with swivel clips fas-tened around the opening with small screws. Predrill the holes and place the clips every 10" or so, making sure they swing out of the way so the panel can be removed and replaced.

22. At this point you can finish the door as desired. Chapter 7 covers paints and finishes and how they pertain to exterior applications. To hang the door, refer to Chapter 17 for specific procedures.

23. Install the door hardware exactly as described in the manufacturer's instructions. A full general explanation of knobs and locksets is included in Chapter 8. For successful weather sealing, you'll need to install a sweep at the bottom rail. Hold the door closed and set the sweep so it's just touching the threshold. Mark the screw holes, then predrill and install the screws. Adjust the sweep within its range as needed, then tighten the screws, taking care not to distort the metal sweep frame.

■ OPTIONS

If you'd prefer this style of door without the kick panels, some minor changes in procedure make it possible. Instead of marking the lower stile tenons for removal, leave them intact. Do not cut a 1/2" mortise into the lock or kick rails, but rather cut profiled tenons at those locations. You may leave the kick rail at a 9-1/2" overall width, but should increase the lock rail to 5" wide overall to maintain a 4" face. Likewise, the center stile should be 5" wide overall and edged each side with profiled tenons rather than 1/2" mortises. The broad tenons at the ends should be replaced with 3/4" mortises.

As a further option, the center stile and even the lock rail can be eliminated entirely to give the door a more open appearance. In this case, the kick rail would need only a tenon.

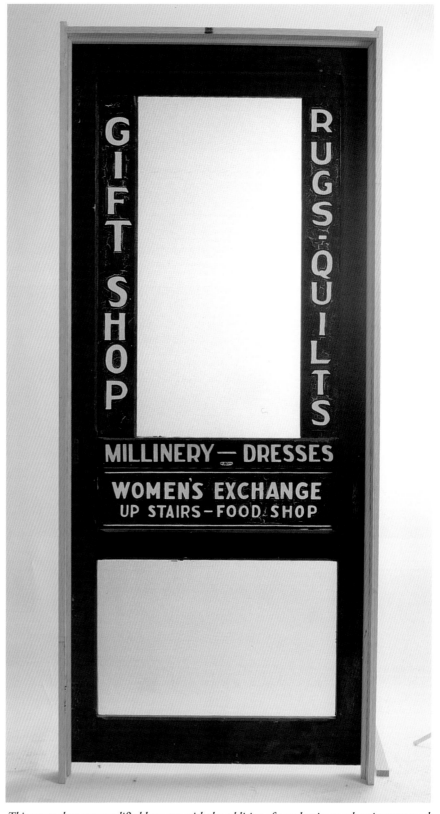

This screen door was modified long ago with the addition of panel strips to advertise store goods.

CHAPTER 16

BISCUIT-JOINED BIFOLD DOOR

> **Overall Dimensions:** 29-3/4" X 80"
> Each 14-3/4" X 80"
>
> **Stock:** White Pine 1-1/2" X 10"
>
> **Stock Finished Size:** 1-3/8" X 4"
> 1-3/8" X 4-1/2"
> 1-3/8" X 7"
> 1-3/8" X 9"
>
> **Style:** Three-panel frame and panel bifold

SUGGESTED TOOLS

Table saw

Biscuit joiner

Router

1/4" X 1/2" slot-cutting bit

Block plane

Straightedge

Tape measure

Try square

Pipe clamps

Hammer

Coping saw

Palm sander

CUT LIST

2	Stiles	1-3/8" X 4-1/2" X 80"
2	Stiles	1-3/8" X 2" X 80"
4	Rails	1-3/8" X 4" X 8-1/4"
2	Lock rails	1-3/8" X 7" X 8-1/4"
2	Kick rails	1-3/8" X 9" X 8-1/4"
2	Top panels	3/4" X 9" X 13-1/2"
2	Mid panels	3/4" X 9" X 18-3/4"
2	Kick panels	3/4" X 9" X 26"

HARDWARE AND SUPPLIES

No. 20 (15/16" X 2-9/16") biscuits

Waterproof aliphatic resin glue

3-leaf hinges

Butt hinges

Knob

I FREQUENTLY GET REQUESTS to build odd-sized doors after homeowners have failed to turn up anything suitable in an off-the-shelf search. I've always been able to please these people aesthetically, but until recently I couldn't keep costs all that competitive because of the time it takes to make a strong joint.

Though I've used dowels in the past, I've never been satisfied with their strength under demanding circum-stances and over time (and quietly hope none have come apart in a client's parlor). But these days there's a tool that's transformed a time-consuming process into mild entertainment and offers a quick-finished joint in the bargain: the biscuit joiner (see page 35).

Biscuit joinery got its start years ago in Switzerland, and I was introduced to the process much later in a small window-and-door manufacturing outfit specializing in European-style windows.

I was assigned the task of designing and producing several large entryways, using a unique profile that included a number of components. The biscuit joiner seemed like the perfect tool for this kind of production work, but I wasn't about to put my faith in the flimsy-looking 4mm-thin oblong wafers used to hold the wood together.

Not knowing better, I put in biscuits by the baker's dozen just to be sure. Later, I had to remove a portion of a door I'd glued up just 15 minutes earlier, and ended up having to saw it apart. From that point on, I used fewer biscuits and gave them ample spacing.

Actually, published research upholds biscuit joining as one of the strongest door-joinery techniques around, but stops short at claiming any long-term success in exterior applications. As for me, I've been using the biscuit tool more and more where appropriate just to be competitive and feel very comfortable as long as I use a high-quality glue in the process.

This bifold door was made to match a set of existing three-panel doors in a home nearby. Because of clearance restrictions in a hallway, the owner wanted the bifold design in order to tuck the door out of the way in the warm months. In the winter, it's often closed to trap heat from a woodstove within the main part of the house.

Though this example is planed to 1-3/8" from 1-1/2" stock, I wouldn't recommend going any less than 1" because the framing gets too flimsy. If you have to duplicate a door, as was the case here, begin by measuring the doors in adjoining rooms to recreate the pattern and to match finishes if needed. If the door is stained, it's important to chose a wood species that resembles the existing doors.

The model for this door had four different rail sizes and a center stile, or mullion. The bifold version has six panels and eight rails. Because the width of the model's top two rails were within 1" of each other, I made these the same size for convenience.

The rough opening was 30" X 81", so with a gap of 1/8" on each edge and 1/2" each at top and bottom, the finished unit was planned at 29-3/4" X 80". To keep the door proportional, I made the stiles 4-1/2" wide and the center stile 4" in width, which—when ripped—yielded two 2" stiles, hinge-joined with an unobtrusive 1/4" gap included.

BISCUIT-JOINTED BIFOLD DOOR

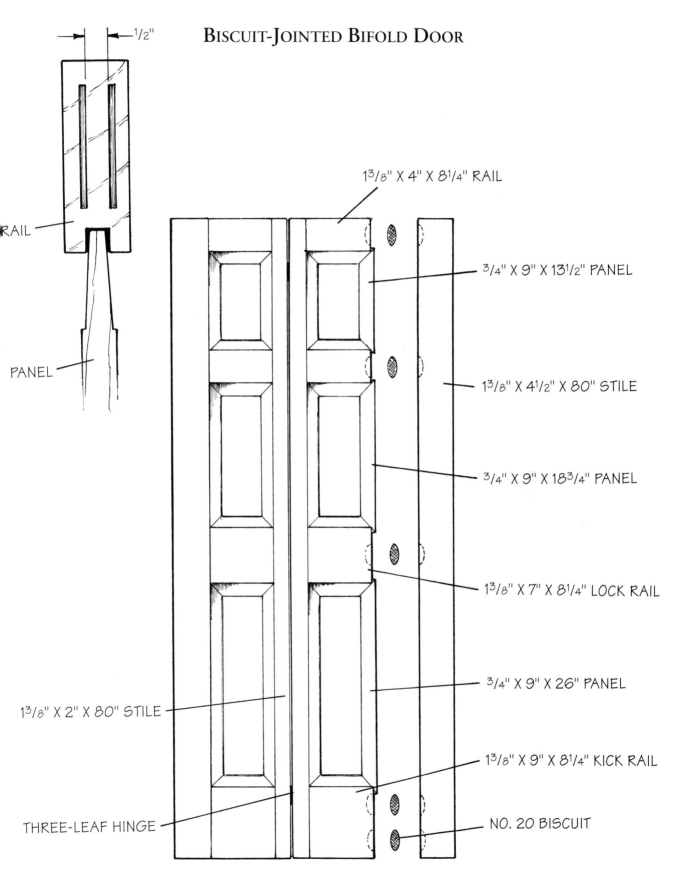

1/2"

RAIL

PANEL

1³/₈" X 4" X 8¹/₄" RAIL

³/₄" X 9" X 13¹/₂" PANEL

1³/₈" X 4¹/₂" X 80" STILE

³/₄" X 9" X 18³/₄" PANEL

1³/₈" X 7" X 8¹/₄" LOCK RAIL

³/₄" X 9" X 26" PANEL

1³/₈" X 2" X 80" STILE

1³/₈" X 9" X 8¹/₄" KICK RAIL

THREE-LEAF HINGE

NO. 20 BISCUIT

Though it would seem to make sense to build this project as one door, then rip it down the center as an assembly, that's not how it's done. If that were the case, the center-stile joints would be perpendicular to those of the outer stiles and the center hinges would be fastened into end grain, causing the screws to pull out eventually.

Once the width of the stiles is established, it's a simple matter to figure the width of the panels and to draw up a cut list for the entire project.

CONSTRUCTION PROCEDURE

1. Begin by planing the framing stock to thickness or having it done at a local shop. Then rip the frame members—rails and stiles—to width (Fig. 1), and cut them to exact length. Turn the stiles inside edge up and use a tape or marking gauge and a straightedge to draw two proportionately spaced lines down the edge of each piece. (On a 1-3/8" surface, the lines would be about 1/2" apart.) Then draw a line down the center of each member. Repeat this procedure on the ends of the rail members (except for the centerline), taking care to maintain the alignment of the marked lines to save heavy sanding later.

2. Mark the locations for each biscuit set by laying up each door and making a line across the face of both rail and stile. The joiner has an indicator on its fence that will register against this mark for perfect accuracy. All the rails should have two biscuits per joint except for the kick rail, which needs a pair at the top and bottom. Adjust the height and depth of the biscuit joiner and complete all the upper cuts, keeping the tool fence square and flat to the work. Then re-adjust the tool for the lower cuts and complete those. Dry-fit the joints but don't force a biscuit into place because it may be difficult to remove.

3. Lay out the doors individually and lightly clamp each one together. Use a 1/4" X 1/2" slot-cutting bit in the router to cut above the marked centerline all around the inside edges of each panel opening (Fig. 2). Then flip the doors over and repeat the process from the other side, which will complete a 1/2" X 1/2" slot for each panel. Double-check the height and width measurements for the panels, remembering to allow 1/8" or so floating room.

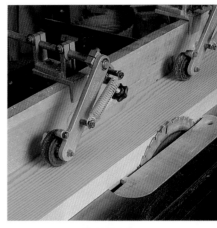

FIGURE 1

FIGURE 2

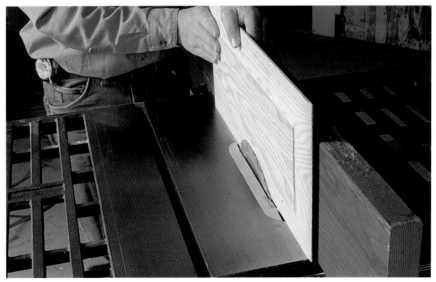

FIGURE 3

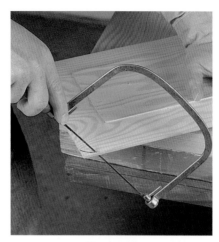

FIGURE 4

FIGURE 5

4. Cut your panels to size from a single width of 1-by material. If that's not possible, use narrower pieces and run the edges through a jointer before gluing up and clamping the stock to make the width you require. If the panel is particularly wide (over 12") use biscuits to hold the joints together.

5. Set up the table saw to cut the panels' beveled edges (Fig. 3). Having a large (or tall auxiliary) fence, a sharp blade, and a small gap in the throat plate will improve your work considerably. Gauge the thickness from the point at which the panel enters the slot, which should be approximately 1/2" in from the outer perimeter. Set the blade angle (which may vary from 5 to 15 degrees or more depending upon the thickness of your stock) and adjust the saw fence accordingly. This cut is made from the opposite side of the blade so the back of the board runs flat against the fence; for the second cut on the double-faced panel, extra care is needed to hold the flat center of the cut panel squarely against the fence. Run a test piece first to check your adjustments

and to gauge any blade marks. They can be corrected by aligning the fence perfectly parallel to the blade.

6. Round the corners from the panels with a sander or coping saw (Fig. 4). Sand the panels carefully (especially at the bevel cuts) and prepare them for finishing if you're concerned about a finish line showing. Finish or prime the wood if you'll be painting it.

7. Disassemble the frames and round over the ends of the rails and the inside edges of the stiles with a sander to enhance the joints. Then lay out all the pieces for assembly, one door at a time. Glue the biscuit slots and biscuits on one stile (Fig. 5) and spread any excess glue on the face of the joints and the exposed half of each biscuit. Glue up the ends of each rail and press them in place against the stile (Fig. 6). Slide the panels into position and glue the remaining biscuits into the other stile. Apply glue to the exposed rail ends and fit the stile into place (Fig. 7). Clamp the door together at each rail and check for square by measuring diagonally

FIGURE 6

FIGURE 7

from corner to corner. Wipe any excess glue from the joints with a damp rag (Fig. 8), and go on to glue up the second door.

8. Size the door halves to the opening, then complete the sanding process (Fig. 9), ending with 220-grit or finer paper if needed for a natural finish. Paint finishes will require a 120-grit sanding to give the coating some "tooth" to adhere to. Finish the door as planned (see Chapter 7).

9. Install the joint hinges carefully to assure that both halves of the door are aligned and even. Because of its integrity, the whole door can be hung on butt hinges if desired without an intrusive track. Lock hardware isn't normally used, but some type of fixed knob or handle can be installed.

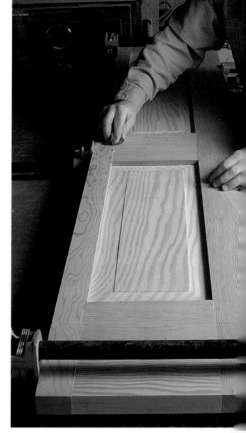

FIGURE 8

■ OPTIONS

If you want to use a flat panel on this type of door, it's a simple matter to cut a centered 1/2" rabbet into the edges of the panel stock rather than beveling the panels. You may also choose to bevel only one side of the panel, leaving the other on the same plane as the shoulder of the slot. The reveal can then be covered with stock trim from the lumber yard, or an appropriate molding can be made with a router and profiled bits.

Determine the distance from the panel to the surface of the door and set the trim so the stop will drop slightly below the surface to create a small reveal. This will not only enhance detail, but also minimizes the irregularities that usually occur when a perfect fit is attempted against a floating panel and a sharp edge. To fit the trim, miter one end and hold it in position, then mark in pencil where the next miter is to go so as not to confuse the direction of cut. Repeat this procedure until all four pieces are fit, then secure them with small finish nails after predrilling the clearance holes

FIGURE 9

THE BEST FIT

CHAPTER 17

INSTALLING AND ADJUSTING A DOOR

HANGING A DOOR can be quite a challenge, as every opening has its own eccentricity. Building custom doors or fitting doors in older homes usually entails making custom jambs to fit the varying circumstances.

If all things were equal, it would be better to build your own jambs from scratch in every circumstance—but economics plays a major role in door-hanging as with most everything else, so prehung door units are mentioned here in passing just so you'll know how they're set in place.

INSTALLING PREHUNG DOORS

A prehung door is like a box frame with a door already hinged to it. The least expensive of the economy prehung doors can cost less than what a skilled craftsman would charge to fabricate the jamb. Prehung doors come in a wide variety of styles and jambs, but regardless of their design, most are quite flimsy and need to be handled with care until they're actually nailed into place. Some have an expandable jamb that makes life easier when wall thicknesses vary, but in practice, they're temperamental and difficult to control when extended all the way.

When ordering prehung units, you'll need to know the style, grade, level of hardware preparation, handing, jamb width, and, of course, the door height and width. An easy way to keep the handing straight is to think of standing in the doorway with your back to the hinge side. If the door swings to

Previous page: Quarter-sawn oak and embellished flat panels within a similarly embellished and slightly raised border panel define the side doors of the Biltmore House Banquet room.

A doorway's rough opening determines how a door will be sized and fitted.

your left, it's a left-handed door; if it swings to the right, a right-handed door. Hardware handing does not necessarily follow this principle so check with your supplier to determine that, especially with handicap or specialty hardware that may not be reversible. Prehung doors come in many grades, from hollow-core up to expensive veneered units.

It pays to use higher-quality hardware and have the setback clearly established if you plan to have the manufacturer prepare the doors. In figuring wall thickness, you can count on having a degree of variance in the common 2 X 4 wall, which will come to about 4-9/16" with 1/2" drywall on both sides. Many door manufacturers use a 4-5/8" standard, which helps cover this thickness discrepancy.

The door will probably come attached to its hinges and have a nail or two on the lock side that needs to be removed, along with the hinge pins. Once the door is free, you'll see how truly flimsy the jamb is, and you'll probably want to tack a brace board, cut to the same width as the head, near the bottom of the side jambs. Your rough opening should allow 1/4" to 1/2" around the jamb perimeter for shimming.

Using a level, check the rough opening's jack studs, or trimmers, for plumb, and the header and floor for level. If the studs are out of plumb by more than 1/4", you'll need to reset them. The trimmers may also be twisted, and you should note the degree and location for later adjustment—they can often be brought straight using shims.

Determine what kind of flooring is going to be used. If it's carpet, you can aim on leaving the side jambs on the subfloor, but if hardwood or tile is planned, the jambs need to rest on that surface. Figure out the thickness of the surface and cut off the bottoms of the jambs by that amount. Then, make up blocks equal to this distance and set

them where the jamb sides will rest.

Now stand the jamb in the door opening and temporarily shim the sides, using no nails. To shim, a pair of tapered shingle sections are driven from each side of the frame between the trimmer studs and the jambs to make a firm rectangular wedge.

Check the head jamb for level, and shim up the low side if needed to achieve that goal. Then transfer the thickness of the shim to the opposite jamb and cut that amount off.

With the head jamb level, plumb the hinge-side jamb by installing shims, starting next to the lower hinge and moving to the upper hinge. If your stud is twisted, you can favor both shims from the widest side.

At this point, you can check the consistency of the jamb width with a spreader. Make one from scrap plywood, or use the lower brace, which can now be removed. Measure the head from inside to inside and cut the spreader to this dimension, then run it down the jamb to ensure that you're allowing enough clearance along its full length. With that established, shim between the top and bottom hinges, then tack the hinge side in part way using three 10-penny finishing nails placed where the stop molding will cover.

Now check to make sure that the wall surface is lined up with the jamb. Hang the door on its hinges and re-check the hinge jamb to see that it's plumb and that there's an even reveal exposed along its edge.

Next, shim and nail the latch jamb at the same approximate locations, allowing a 1/8" to 3/16" gap between the door and the jamb, which can be adjusted by tapping the wedges in or out. Set all the nails below the surface of the wood and trim off the shims by scoring and snapping them, or by cutting. At this point, the door stop can be installed, starting at the hinge side and working around to the head and latch

jamb, mitering the corners and making sure that there's even contact with the closed door all around the perimeter. You can allow up to 1/16" clearance between the door and the stop if desired to compensate for paint. Fasten with a 4-penny nail every 12".

If the door isn't prepared for hardware, a template for installing the latch should be in the hardware kit you purchase. The latch is positioned 36" to 38" above the floor, or at the lock rail if there is one.

Once the knob and latch are in place, close the door and mark the top and bottom of the latch where it contacts the jamb. Measure back to where the latch stops, and position the strike plate accordingly. If it's a dead-latching type of bolt, be sure the guard plunger won't drop into the strike opening when the door's closed. Outline the strike plate with a pencil or sharp knife, then remove the waste material with a chisel to the depth required. Use an auger to bore the bolt opening, which can be squared up with a narrow chisel.

With the hardware in place, install the casing. Leave a 1/4" margin around all the jamb edges and miter the corners on shaped moldings (flat moldings should be butt joined). Set the casing in place with 6-penny finishing nails placed every 16".

An exterior prehung door is installed with the threshold in place, and sometimes a sill is required as well. A sill slopes away from the base of the door to shed water, and the threshold seals the gap between the lower edge of the door and the floor. Often the sill and threshold are milled from a single piece of lumber. The top of the sill should be flush with the finished floor, though sometimes it rests on top of the subfloor and is then flush with the threshold. In any case, it's important that these component are level in order to achieve a good-fitting door. They're fastened to the floor joists with 10-penny finishing nails.

How a Door Fits in Place

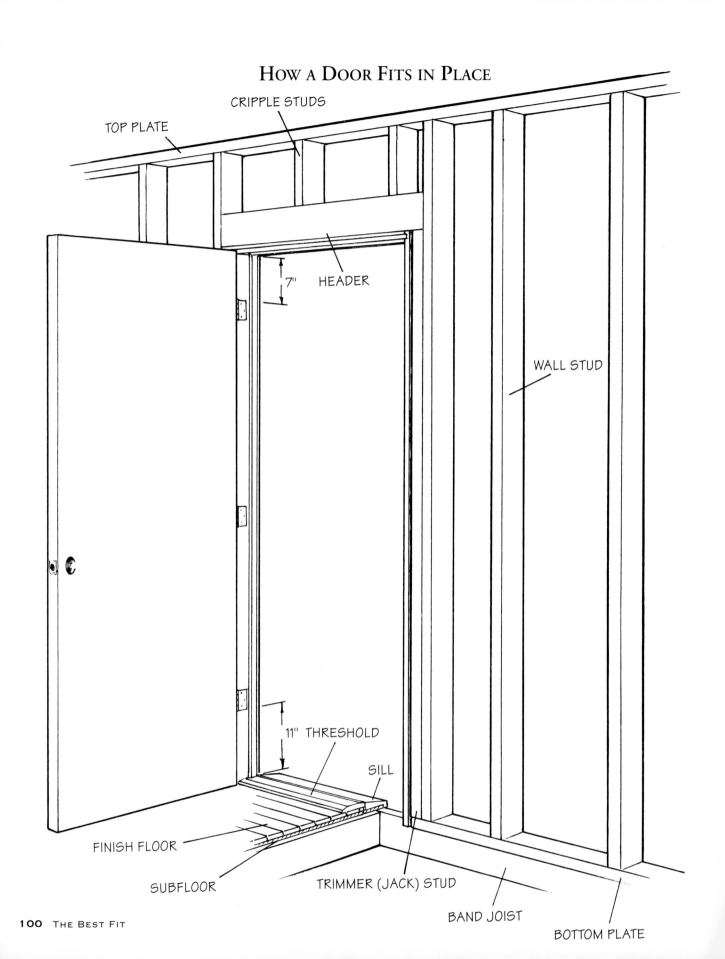

CRIPPLE STUDS

TOP PLATE

7"

HEADER

WALL STUD

11" THRESHOLD

SILL

FINISH FLOOR

SUBFLOOR

TRIMMER (JACK) STUD

BAND JOIST

BOTTOM PLATE

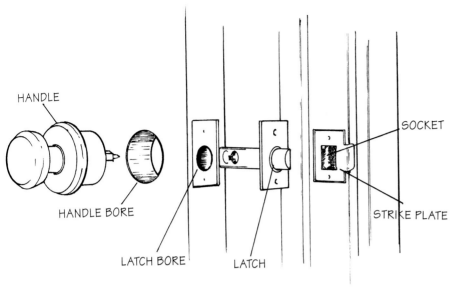

HANDLE

HANDLE BORE

LATCH BORE

LATCH

SOCKET

STRIKE PLATE

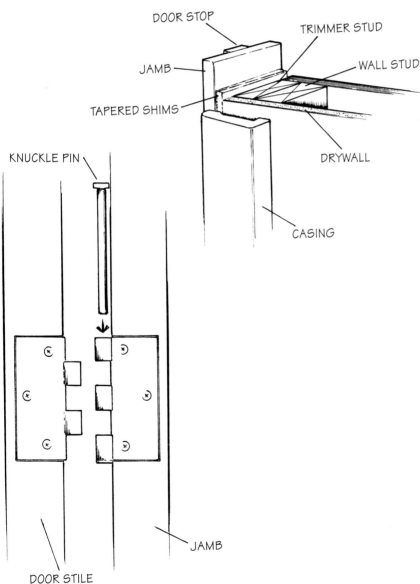

DOOR STOP

JAMB

TAPERED SHIMS

TRIMMER STUD

WALL STUD

DRYWALL

CASING

KNUCKLE PIN

JAMB

DOOR STILE

BUILT JAMBS AND DOORS

Building jambs goes hand in hand with building doors. The ability to make your own jambs also allows you the freedom of choosing salvaged period doors to install (see Chapter 12). Often, when doors are salvaged from old homes and buildings, the jambs are left behind and ultimately destroyed, so they must be recreated.

It's best to use 5/8" or thicker clear pine jamb stock. If you plan to finish the jambs to match the doors, however, it's a good idea to use the same kind of wood if possible.

You'll first need to establish the dimensions of the rough opening to calculate what jamb thickness you can get by with. For interior doors, 4/4 material planed to 3/4" will do well. On exterior work, 6/4 stock brought down to 1" is fine as long as the door isn't exceptionally large or heavy.

The jamb width will depend on how thick your finished walls are. For the standard 2 X 4 stud wall faced with drywall, a 4-5/8" jamb works well, and some lumber suppliers even carry 5/8" X 4-5/8" jamb stock for this purpose.

When assembling jambs, cutting operations will include making dadoes to seat the head jamb between the side jambs, and cutting mortises to seat the hinges. In production work, routers set up with templates are very effective, but with one-at-a-time carpentry, a fine-toothed backsaw and a sharp chisel work quite well. Combined with a try square and a marking gauge, they make cuts and placement very accurate.

Plan ahead for your hardware. For a period look, local salvage and antique shops sometimes have good solid ball-tip hinges and sound old locksets. If not, you can order sturdy square-cornered hinges and a quality lockset from a hardware supplier. Determine the size and type of hinge by the door width, weight, and clearance (see Chapter 8). If you plan to install a dead-bolt lock in addition to the knob lock, be sure that the backset—the distance between the center of the knob and the latch plate—is the same for each unit so the locks will line up vertically on the face of the door.

LOCATING AND CUTTING DADOES

Starting with two pieces of jamb stock, mark the height of the door plus clearance for a rug or threshold. Add a mark above the first at a distance equal to the thickness of the head jamb, and extend both marks across the width of the stock with a try square to mark the dadoes. Cut off the ends of the jambs 3/4" to 1" above the dado marks.

Then clamp the pieces to the top of the workbench alongside each other and mark the depth of the cut, which should be at least half the thickness of each jamb. Use a backsaw or router with fence to cut to the first line. Hold up the head jamb to double-check the thickness, then cut to the second line. If you're using a saw, make repeated cuts between the lines to remove the waste, then clean the bottom of the cut with a chisel.

LOCATING THE HINGES

When installing a door that has hinges intact, or has mortises already cut for hinges, lay the jamb on the door edge, leaving a 1/16" gap between the top of the door and the head jamb mortise cut. Mark each existing hinge location on the edge of the jamb.

If the hinges or mortises are not already on the door, lay out the upper edge of the top hinge 7" down from the head mortise and the lower edge of the bottom hinge 11" up from the bottom of the jamb. Then center the middle hinge an equal distance from the top and bottom hinges.

The usual distance from the back edge of the hinge to the stop location is 5/16", with a distance of 1/4" from that edge to the door's edge. This leaves 1/16" clearance between the stop and the edge of the door for paint and sea-

sonal swelling. Mark the thickness of the hinges on the edge of the jamb with a sharp knife, and score around the hinges to mark with the blade.

CHISELING MORTISES

When working with only a door or two, a chisel seems the best tool to cut out mortises because it avoids the trouble of setting up a router with a hinge template and all the accessories. Using a 1"-wide chisel, sharply drive the edge down into the wood with the bevel facing inward at both ends of the mortise. You can score the back edge with a sharp knife, or carefully tap the chisel. Then make a series of cuts inside the mortise area at right angles to the edge of the jamb, tilting the chisel slightly toward the beveled edge.

Next, chisel out the series of chips in the opposite direction, then clean up the surface by holding the chisel flat on the surface. Check the fit with the hinge in place, and pare down any high spots. Mark the screw holes with a pencil and use an awl to center-mark a small bit before drilling.

ASSEMBLING AND FITTING THE FRAME

Cut the head jamb the width of the door, the depth of the two side jamb mortises, plus 1/4" for the reveal around the door. Mark the center of the back of each mortise on the jamb to align the screws, and predrill two 3/32" holes to keep from splitting the wood. Assemble the components and fasten them together with No. 6 X 1-1/2" screws.

Then, cut two spreaders from scrap to a length equal to the outer width of the assembled frame, placing one near the center and the other a foot or so up from the bottom. These are temporary, to help keep things together in fitting, and can be secured with 4-penny finishing nails.

To fit the frame, center it in the rough opening and push shims between the side jambs and the jack studs at the

location of the hinges, on both sides. Use a long level to check for plumb on the sides and level on the head jamb (if you don't have a long level, you can make-do by holding a smaller level against a long, straight section of board). Adjust the shims to compensate for any warps and bows in the studs, then fasten the frame into the rough opening, following the procedure described in "Installing Prehung Doors," above.

ADJUSTING DOORS

Door-hanging experience comes from many places, and each facet contains something unique. There's a variety of techniques professionals use to achieve the same result, and those whose business is doors always like to experiment with new ones.

One of the greatest challenges in door adjustment comes when a building has some years on it, and may have not only gone through some abuse and "remuddling," but has conceded somewhat to the inevitable effects of settling. Even newer structures can have problems keeping still, or may have never been square and plumb to begin with.

This is where the Zen of door adjustment applies. It's practiced by putting yourself in a semiconscious state, standing back from the door in question, and telling yourself: "I will do everything possible to make adjustments before I will plane or cut off any part of this door."

In a practical sense, that means looking at the reveal around the perimeter of the door for any inconsistency. If the top of the door is sticking around the lock stile and you have more than 1/8" between the stile and the jamb, you may be able to shim out the top hinge by loosening the hinge screws a few turns on either the door or jamb and fitting a scrap of cardboard, cut to the length of the hinge and perhaps 1/4" wide, behind it with a push or two from a straight-bladed screwdriver.

Tighten the screws—back one first—and check the door. If it's no longer rubbing at the top and just slightly rubbing the side, you can try a thinner shim. On the other hand, if the adjustment was not enough, you can double the thickness by cutting a wider piece and scoring it before folding it over.

If there's a good-sized gap on the butt edge of the door, you can loosen the bottom leaf and place a similar shim at the very back of the mortise—away from the knuckle—then tighten the front screws first, thus canting the door back toward the butt jamb.

This technique can be used in opposite fashion by using shims on both hinges and building the door out equally to keep the butt edge from compressing on the jamb and binding the door.

By using such shims in the appropriate combinations, you can gain quite a bit of control of your door. You may also find that deepening the mortises on the jamb or the door has a similar effect—but it must be done with care, because you can easily overcompensate by making too great an adjustment at once.

If it becomes apparent that the door does need trimming—for instance, the entire front edge is sticking and moisture, temperature, or finish isn't the reason—always plane the hinged edge. You can easily adjust the depth of the hinges, but not the lockset. If needed, you can bevel the lock stile's leading edge 5 degrees or so to help the door clear the jamb, then slightly round over the door's edges for a good feel.

Remember when trimming the top or bottom that the end grain of the stiles will have a tendency to tear out, especially in planing. Always plane toward the center of the door, starting at one end and working toward the opposite stile, then making a second start from the other side and working to the first point.

Here's a tip for cutting the bottom of an interior door: Scribe a pencil mark along the bottom of the door when it's shut, then check for any high spots on the floor by swinging the door out and taking measurements.

To remove the door, drive out the hinge pins with a few hammer taps to a straight-bladed screwdriver held on the edge of the finial or the top of the pin. Some pins can be driven out from the bottom, but be aware that some decorative ball tips are screwed in place rather than compression fit.

Once the door is off its hinges, lay it down on a flat surface that will allow you some control when cutting. You can clamp a straightedge to the door as a guide, setting it back from the cut line to the offset of your saw's bottom plate. Protect the finish by applying masking tape to the surface of the door where the plate rides, and even over the cut line itself to prevent fraying its edges. Use a sharp blade and set it to a depth just a little more than the thickness of the door. Move slowly, especially at the ends where tearout can occur.

Rehanging the door is a good job for two people, but can be done single-handedly in a pinch by using a 6" block about the thickness of the door's reveal when it's open. Place the block at the midpoint of where the door would be if it were open 45 degrees, then with pins in hand, bring the door up and rest it on the block so it teeters under your control easily. Rock the door back and forth to get it to match the top hinge, then slide the pin in. Raise the bottom of the door enough to remove the block and set the lower hinge in place, then slide that pin in.

Occasionally a door binds on its stop, and you can sometimes drive the stop back a bit using a mallet and a length of 1 X 6. Some older doors might have a built-in internal stop, in which case this adjustment doesn't apply.

Warped doors pose a whole different problem. To check for warpage, hold a long straightedge along the leading edge of the door on both sides and note the degree of deviation. In some cases, the stops can be removed and simply repositioned. If the door is away from the stop at the top and in contact at the bottom, you can adjust the bottom hinge out from its original position 1/4" or so by drilling new pilot holes and screwing the hinge down in its new place.

There is another technique that could be tried to correct a warped door, though it's often carried out with limited success. Remove the door from its hinges and place it flat between two saw horses, convex side up. Load up the face with weight until you've over-compensated for the warp by a factor of no more than 25%. Dampening the door will sometimes aid this process. Be warned that this procedure can damage the door's joinery, so it's to be used only as a last resort. Also, old doors tend to retain a memory of where they want to be and often return there. If the correction was successful, sealing the wood properly may help prevent a relapse since moisture is the most common cause of warpage.

The start of any installation is to establish a level floor and head jamb. The frame members at each side need to be plumb as well.

After the hinge mortises are cut and the jamb is built, the assembly is slipped into position.

Close shim spacing assures that the frame of this heavy side-paneled entry door won't migrate with the daily traffic it's sure to experience.

Head casing is installed with 6-penny finishing nails, allowing a small reveal at the edge of the jamb.

The mortise for a hinge leaf is initially cut to the scribed outline in a series of slices with a chisel.

A sharp spade bit removes waste from the mortise swiftly; the depth of the bore and center alignment must be checked often.

The outline for the face plate of the mortise lock is scribed deeply with a sharp knife.

Cutting the mortise to the depth of the plate requires good judgement and a careful hand.

The mortise unit houses a separate lock and cylinder. It's fastened to the wood above and below the mortise itself.

Three large, ball-tipped hinges are needed to support the heavy oak door. They are positioned, scribed, and mortised prior to assembling the jamb.

The finished door and entryway. The side panels are designed to complement the door style.

CHAPTER 18

ENTRYWAYS

Massive steel portal doors enclose quarter-sawn oak entry doors at the vestibule of the Basilica of St. Lawrence DM.

Up until some point in the late seventeenth century, homes were generally modest structures with a single front entrance. But as individuals began to flourish in the rich agricultural economy of the New World, houses became larger and grander and took on the embellishments of prosperity. Single entrances became formal front doors and those developed into exquisite front entryways as other means of access were added.

Pediments, pilasters, and scrollwork offered a classic touch; fanlights and sidelights admitted light to an otherwise windowless hallway; larger openings and even double doors attested to the prominence of the owner.

These are important architectural elements to be sure, and it's important to include them in the design of a new door, or even your best efforts at joinery can go wasted. A common mistake in renovation, especially when it comes to doors, is to become captivated by the door itself and to ignore the architecture surrounding it. The result is a door that simply does not fit into the theme of the entryway, even though it may be a perfect fit within its frame.

Even a minimum of research, a few hours spent perusing architectural history books or even pictures of old houses, can impart a sense of continuity in the various architectural styles. The doorbuilder who can successfully tie in the new door to the existing elements of the old will have made his or her work notable. If you have the original door available to copy from, your work is half done. But even if you're starting from scratch, you can carry existing features through to accentuate and complete the whole facade.

Left: This circa-1911 cottage has a recessed doorway and a simply embell-ished covered entryway. Both combine to keep the effects of weather from the door while adding aesthetic appeal.

Above: A late 19th-century home now used as an office was built with a covered stoop which carries the character of some Victorian elements and keeps rain and sun off the double doors.

Below: George W. Vanderbilt's Biltmore House shows how ornate an entry-way can be. Marble, mahogany, and stained glass are well-protected beneath a domed, brick-faced portfolio.

Where and how a door is situated will also dictate its features. An entryway exposed to direct sunlight and weather has a difficult time protecting a door. Fragile finishes are out of the question, and wood movement becomes prob-lematic as joints and trimwork lose their integrity.

If at all possible, a door should enjoy some degree of safekeeping, as its life is hard enough. But if that's not possible, compensation may have to be made at the design stage to avoid trouble later on. This includes allowing for expan-sion in paneled doors and taking care in fitting during installation. It may also mean limiting finishes to only the paints and varnishes that can withstand the worst the weather can throw at it.

A two-paned glass French door bought as salvage and adapted to the existing opening for The New French Bar cafe.

Previous page: An arched-top portal gate shows the combination of a simple frame-and-batten style with open spindles. Hammered-iron offset hinges and a single latch stop let the door swing inward.

The transom glass is matched to the center light on this Arts and Crafts style frame and panel door.

Above left: This glass-paned door was embellished with a hand-painting technique (see p.43) to welcome customers to Touchstone Gallery.

Above: An otherwise simple design benefits from the bolection moldings around the panels of this door, the front entry of a home built in 1883. Note the use of the astragal as a stop molding and weather seal.

Left: The home shows its Charleston influence through the use of this unusual vertical pocket window—built so both sashes are fully concealed in an upper cavity when opened, thus avoiding a period tax on doors.

George W. Vanderbilt's bedroom bath door at Biltmore House is defined by a formal architrave incorporating stepped pedestal, column, carved capital, and intricate frieze work.

Above left: This service-station door, circa 1930, was rescued as salvage. Complex as it looks, it could be recreated without much difficulty in the home shop.

Above: Six-light glazing above a beaded-panel frame-and-batten design identifies this X-braced, or crossbuck, private fire-station door. The drop latch is typical of period utility hardware.

Left: Incorporating a curved-edge top rail into a traditional frame permits the suggestion of an arched door without suffering the toil of redesigning the opening. The battens are tongue-and-groove, the wood heart pine.

Above: Single-glaze art glass set in a white pine frame. There are a variety of methods for bedding and glazing stained glass.

Above right: Cut glass and a decorative ledge mark this entry door as distinctive. The raised panel floats behind a bead molding.

Right: A set of embellished twin doors with raised circular panels. The adornment around the glass panels is a good example of period appliqué.

Above: The arched entryway houses a set of heavy oak six-panel rectangular doors. Massive full-width iron strap hinges provide its support.

Above right: A unique door and window treatment. The two-panel door does not provide egress to the roof, but access to storage space beneath the eaves.

George W. Vanderbilt's Billiard Room incorporates hidden panel doors with touch-activated knobless latches which lead to other chambers within the wing.

A slight curvature of the head molding and kick rail of this Biltmore House door betrays its position in a circular Tower Room. The linen-fold panel carving is a bedroom door theme.

This simple pine pantry door set owes its character to the ten horizontal panels and the use of an architrave with embellished corner blocks.

A five-panel Colonial design and prominent bolection molding differentiate this panel door from other typical panel styles.

Above: A traditional two-part stable door with heavy frames and tongue-and-groove panels. Surface-mounted strap hinges were fitted at the frames' unchamfered corners.

Above right: A far-from-traditional stable door in a Biltmore Estate archway, suspended from a track. The stiles and top rails house massive let-in arch rails to match the door opening. A panel and cross-buck pattern is used below.

Right: Another arched-door treatment, this for a city firehouse designed by Douglas Ellington and built around 1927. These are four individual frame-and-panel doors, center-hinged in sets and hung at the stiles. V-grooved and full-beveled panels are used.

Left: Doug Johnston's handmade "sunburst" door uses biscuit-joined 7/4" pine framing and 1/2" tongue-and-groove panel inserts against a 3/4" core.

Below left: The alternating diagonal pattern and the vertical pattern used in the hallway door at left are 3/4" strips backed against a 1/4" foundation panel and framed in 7/4" pine.

Below: Both chevron-patterned doors are assembled with a biscuit-joined frame and use 3/4" tongue-and-groove face panels against a foundation panel within a 1-3/4" frame.

Above: Another Arts and Crafts door with stained glass transom and light. Note the door's shortened stiles, extreme width, and the matching color in trim and panels. Wide doors allowed passage of bulky Craftsman furniture.

Above right: A distinctive surface-batten detail on a Craftsman-style pantry door. The vertical battens both cover and help secure the joints.

Right: Hand-hammered hardware is right at home on this rustic outbuilding door. The loop latch is typical of period closures.

Above: A simple linear-panel door with single light.
The panels are true raised cuts with a concave bead.

Left: This oval-light beveled-glass door dates from circa 1870
and uses mill-turned appliqués over a false-grain oak panel.

Opposite panel designs adorn the walnut Library doors at Biltmore House. A book-leaf pattern to the outside, and carvings by Karl Bitter.

The Breakfast Room door shows a unique flat panel-on-panel design and an unusually large field. The Italian marble casing carries through to the wainscoting.

Refurbished by the author, these two-panel twins are characterized by their patterned mullions.
They were made right- and left-handed for the sake of symmetry.

This entryway demonstrates true functional side windows as opposed to fixed sidelights.
The oak door is characteristic of the Arts and Crafts style, flat-paneled with a traditional latch set.

The four-panel door on this built-in-place kast closet has a mitered, unadorned casing and a clear varnish finish.

Some judicious trim adjustments allowed this standard-sized five-panel door to fit in a rather tight spot beneath the stairs.

Left: A set of wide double-Z frame-and-panel batten doors at this historic Biltmore Industries building. The diagonal bracing is reversed on the left door, either in error or for aesthetic reasons.

Below left: The full-raised panels and detail work on the frames around them is perfect for a twelve-panel door. Note the embellishments on the casing and transom frame.

Below: This cottage door is a functional two-piece, or Dutch, door with leaded glass and sidelights.

GLOSSARY

APPLIQUÉ. An embellishment added onto a door panel or framework for decoration or to provide period adornment. Often used in combination with moldings and carved or turned pieces for effect.

ARCHITRAVE. The finish molding around a door opening. It may consist of tapered sections mitered at the upper corners, or take the form of fluted rectangular-section pieces decorated with square, embellished blocks nailed into the corners.

ASTRAGAL. A piece of T-molding fastened to the edge of the inactive door on a set of double doors which functions as the stop for the active door.

BACKSET. The distance from the face plate of the latch assembly to the centerline of the lock cylinder.

BARREL. The cylindrical hollow section positioned between the leaves of a hinge to receive the pin. It's also referred to as the knuckle.

BISCUIT. A manufactured spline used in a power biscuit joiner to complete a machined biscuit joint.

BLIND TENON. A tenon that does not protrude through the joint and thus is not exposed at the opposite edge.

BOLECTION. A molding which separates two planes and projects beyond the surfaces of both. Usually used between a panel and a rail or stile.

BUCK. The crossed framing pieces in a cross-buck panel door.

CAPITAL. The upper support elements of a column on a formal entryway.

CASING. Trim or molding that covers the space between the finish door frame, or jamb, and the wall.

COLUMN. One of the two posts or shafts that define the right and left limits of a formal entryway.

COPE. The curved edge of a frame-member cut or a piece of molding incorporating a concave surface.

CRIPPLE. A short stud placed between a door header and the top plate when framing rough openings.

CYLINDER. The part of a lock that contains the keyhole and tumbler mechanism.

DADO. A rectangular slot cut across the grain of a wooden member.

DENTIL. A strip of molding consisting of a series of rectangular blocks projecting from the surface.

DOWEL. A wooden pin fit into holes drilled into adjoining frame members to create a dowel joint.

ESCUTCHEON. A decorative metal plate secured against the door face behind the knob and lock.

FACE PLATE. A metal fitting attached to the latch unit which is mortised into the door and fastened to hold the latch assembly in place. Also known as a mounting plate.

FANLIGHT. The glass panel set into the radiused opening above a formal entryway.

FIELD. The smooth center surface of a raised panel.

FLUSH DOOR. A door with a flat surface, consisting of plywood or hardboard face panels glued to an internal frame.

GROOVE. A slot cut lengthwise along the grain of a wooden member, usually to receive the tongue of a matching board.

HEADER. A wooden member placed across the top of a rough door opening in a framed wall to support weight from overhead. Also referred to as a lintel.

HINGE. A metal fixture with one or more movable joints that fastens between the door and the jamb to allow the door to swing.

HOLLOW-CORE. A type of flush door that uses a mesh or cell core to provide backing for the face panels.

JAMB. The finish frame of a door opening, consisting of the head jamb at the top, side jambs, and the threshold at the bottom.

KICK PLATE. A metal or composite plate mounted to the lower door rail or face to prevent foot damage to the surface or structure of a high-traffic door.

LATCH BOLT. A retractable pin or bar that is the part of the lockset that meets the strike plate and secures the door in a closed position.

LEAF. The flat pieces of a door hinge, fastened onto the door and jamb with screws.

LIGHT. A glass pane in a door or window.

LINTEL. A wooden member placed across the top of a rough door opening in a framed wall to support weight. Similar to a header, but usually cut from a single piece of wood.

LOCKSET. The entire lock unit, consisting of the locks, strike plate, latch bolt, and trim pieces.

MORTISE. An opening cut into a frame member to receive a matching tenon from another member, together creating a mortise-and-tenon joint. A mortise cavity can also receive hardware such as hinges or a lock.

MOUNTING PLATE. A metal plate attached to the latch unit which is mortised into the door and holds the latch in place. Also called a face plate.

MULLION. The vertical center piece of the frame in a panel door, also called the center stile. In a glass panel door, vertical mullions also separate the lights.

MUNTIN. The horizontal pieces that separate the lights in a glass-panel door.

PANEL. A wooden insert that fits between the stiles and rails of a panel door. Panels are usually beveled, routed, or shaped in such a way as to give some definition to the field, as in a raised-panel door.

PEDESTAL. The lower support elements of a column on a formal entryway.

PIN. A finished bolt that holds the two leaves of a hinge together when inserted in the barrel.

PLATE. The horizontal framing member at the top and bottom of a stud-framed wall.

RABBET. An open groove cut along the edge of a wooden member. Also called a rebate.

RAIL. One of the horizontal pieces of the frame in a panel door, consisting of the top rail, lock rail, and kick rail.

REBATE. A variation of the term rabbet, a channel or groove cut along the edge or face of a wooden member.

RECEIVER. A ledge or rebate included at the inside edges of door stiles, rails, or muntins to serve as a bed for screening or glazing.

ROUGH OPENING. A framed opening in a wall sized to accommodate a finished door.

SHIMS. A narrow strip cut from tapered shingles and used in pairs to plumb and straighten door jambs.

SIDELIGHT. One of the glass panels set to either side of a door in a formal entryway.

SILL. A piece of wood butted against the threshold, flooring, and subfloor on some exterior doors. It's milled from a single board and pitched with one bevel at a 2" in 12" ratio.

SOLID CORE. A type of flush door that uses particleboard or blocks set in an alternating pattern to provide backing for the face panels.

SPLINE. A block or strip of wood fit into mortises or grooves cut into adjoining frame members to create a spline-tenon joint.

STICK. A thin wooden strip used to hold a glass pane in place within its rabbet; also called a stop.

STILE. One of the vertical side pieces of the frame in a panel door. The butt stile is at the hinge side and the lock stile at the lockset side.

STOP. A piece of molding installed at the head and side jambs which prevents the door from swinging past the strike plate. Also, a thin wooden strip used to hold a glass pane within its rabbet.

STRIKE PLATE. A metal fitting with a central hole, mortised into the door jamb to receive the latch bolt when the door is closed.

SWEEP. A metal, felt, or rubber strip fastened to the lower edge of an exterior or cold-surface door to seal the gap at the threshold and prevent air and water infiltration.

TENON. The protruding part at the end of a frame member cut to fit within a mortise to create a mortise-and-tenon joint.

THRESHOLD. A metal, wood, or stone piece fastened between the side jambs at the bottom of the door opening. The term saddle is sometimes used to describe an interior threshold with two opposed bevels which spans dissimilar floor surfaces.

THROUGH TENON. A tenon cut to the full width of its adjoining member so its end is exposed at the edge, and the mortise is cut completely through.

TONGUE. The protruding part of a frame or other wooden member cut to fit within a dado or groove.

TRACK. A metal channel fastened to the head jamb to guide the trolley of a bifold door.

TRANSOM. A small opening over a door, usually fitted with a hinged sash or stationary louver.

TRIM RING. A piece of finish hardware secured between the door face and the lock cylinder.

TRIMMER STUD. A vertical framing member nailed to the studs at a rough door opening to support the ends of a header.

TROLLEY. A roller assembly fastened to the second unit of a bifold door and fitted to an overhead track.

WEATHERSTRIP. Metal, felt, or rubber strips fastened at the stop molding of an exterior door to prevent air and water infiltration.

INDEX